CW01475255

THE
MAYS
28

THE MAYS 28

New Writing and Art from the Students of Cambridge and Oxford

VARSITY

GUEST EDITED BY
Oscar Murillo &
Philippe Sands

Varsity Publications Ltd
16 Mill Lane
Cambridge CB2 3RF
United Kingdom

First published 2020 by Varsity Publications Ltd

Varsity Business Manager - Mark Curtis
business@varsity.cam.ac.uk

ISBN 978-0-902240-51-3

Designed and typeset by
Linda Yu

Printed and bound by
Biddles Books

Cover image by
Maria Kaminska

British Library Cataloguing in Publication Data:
A CIP catalogue record of this book is available from the British Library.

Further copies of this book any other titles in the series can be bought through most booksellers or direct from Varsity Publications at the address above or at:
www.varsity.co.uk/themays
www.themaysanthology.co.uk

CONTENTS

CONTENTS

Content Note

Please be advised that the following stories contain:

POTENTIALLY DISCONCERTING DISCUSSIONS OF SEX

Champagne, Trevor

2019: An American Childhood

she wonders how uncommon

DEATH OF A CHILD

The Sun, Our Impermanent Star

EDITING TEAM

EDITOR

Zoë Matt-Williams

DEPUTY EDITOR

Rebekah Rochester

LAYOUT DESIGNER

Linda Yu

ART EDITOR

Gonçalo Albergaria

POETRY EDITOR

Samuel McIlhagga

PROSE EDITOR

Caterina Bragoli

ART COMMITTEE

Alayo Akinkugbe

Anastasia Kolomiets

POETRY COMMITTEE

Ashna Ahmad

Madeleine Constant

Ben Philipps

Neha Usmani

PROSE COMMITTEE

Joshua Askew

Alexandra Germer

Mo Gillani

Jessie Ingram-Johnson

SUBMISSIONS OFFICER

Rachel Weatherley

OXFORD ASSOCIATE EDITOR

Hamza Rana

PUBLICITY AND EVENTS

Eira Elisabeth Murphy

Rachael Rajah

Maya Yousif

FOREWORD

Philippe Sands

What a joy to read the nine prose contribution to the *Mays* in the spring of 2020.

They were delivered at a particular moment. Several days into a period of prolonged isolation, prompted by a virus—'Sars-Cov-2 is the virus, Covid-19 the illness', Paul Giordano explains in his important new essay, 'How Contagion Works'—we are instructed by the authorities to cease external activity. How adaptable we are! How easily we fall into place! Yet how deadly is this moment for some, and how difficult it is for all, not least the generation that has created this fine anthology.

In this way we are called upon to dig deeper into our inner selves, to find sustenance and solace in the basics. Eating and sleeping, other intimacies, thinking and talking, writing and reading.

In writing, I spend much time thinking about the relationship between writer and reader.

The prose writer—fiction and non-fiction alike—engages in an act that draws on personal experience and catalyses a reflection on the impact of such experience. What touches me? What do I care about? How can I make it easier? Who am I?

The reader is engaged by the very same words and their arrangement into a story, but in a different way: the words of the storyteller offer an insight into the experience of another, as does their rendering. In turn, these offer insights that are capable of filling gaps, of helping the reader better to understand their own lives, who they are.

An unspoken conversation occurs. It is a special, momentary relationship. The writer selects words, and chooses to arrange them in a way that offers a particular meaning for them, but cannot impose a particular reaction upon the reader. For the reader arrives at the act of reading with a baggage of their own.

This space, between the desires of the writer, on the one hand, and the reaction of the reader, on the other, is a place of magical experience. When it works, the universe of the imagination opens up. But it is also a momentary experience, one that will soon be replaced by another, and one that is dependent on the context in which it occurs, its time and its place.

My reading of the *Mays* is situated in a moment in which certain words and phrases and their ordering might open up the imagination and the senses.

A theatrical performance is cancelled. A childhood bedroom's special darkness noted. A phone dies. A body is desired. A tongue is examined. A vanilla ice cream melts. A park visit is prepared. A distant life imagined.

How uncommon is this particular moment? I keep returning to the shortest of the pieces, not even one sentence. 'She Wonders How Uncommon' is so evocative, so uncertain, so dangerous, so enticing. We've all been there. From that minute experience it is not a great leap to where we are today.

The magic of writing. Thank you to all and each. ◆

TLV-GV

FLIGHT

FROM

Oscar Murillo

TLV-GYD FLIGHT J2 22

Oscar Murillo

Oscar Murillo guest edited this year's art section, helping select the pieces in collaboration with the committee. Instead of a formal introduction, he has contributed a written piece himself: an exploration of a flight he boarded from Tel Aviv to Baku, during which he realised the presence of a deceased body on board and changes in the plane's flight path to avoid Syrian territories. This experience has since informed his artistic practice, building on these reflections about conflict, collective mourning and empty space.

The tense state of air travel, the distressing experience of a family losing a loved one—the deceased body loaded in the cargo of this Boeing aircraft. Google Maps, FlightMapper and Plane Finder, all tools meant for geographical awareness, which help to illustrate the reality of a region in discontent.

FlightMapper illustrates that upon take-off flight J2 22 should cruise northeastwards crossing Israel, Palestine,

Jordan, Turkey, Iran, and finally arrive in Baku on an uphill diagonal. Nevertheless, as cruising altitude was achieved the aircraft sped further and further over the Mediterranean Sea, passing the northeastern tip of Cyprus, before reaching the middle of Turkey whilst cruising above the town of Tepeköy in the Mersin province, where a right turn directed the aircraft northeast, through northern Turkey and towards Azerbaijan.

Awareness of a deceased body in the cargo compartment, and the rightward turn of this midnight flight opened up an imaginary abstract landscape. It is this rightward turn that shed light on my understanding of dead matter, the void and dark abstract space. My gaze fixed out of the plane window towards mapped neighbouring territories affirmed with certainty that this was perhaps the closest I would come to some kind of annihilated world.

Layers of ivory black oil paint are applied and then burnished into what feels and is experienced as heavy compressed material, time compressed and fossilised to no singular issue, information gathered through investigations with a radical negativity: absorption of the detritus of a failed period. There is nothing left, all has collapsed. Via Google Maps these thoughts materialise whilst tracking the flight. ◆

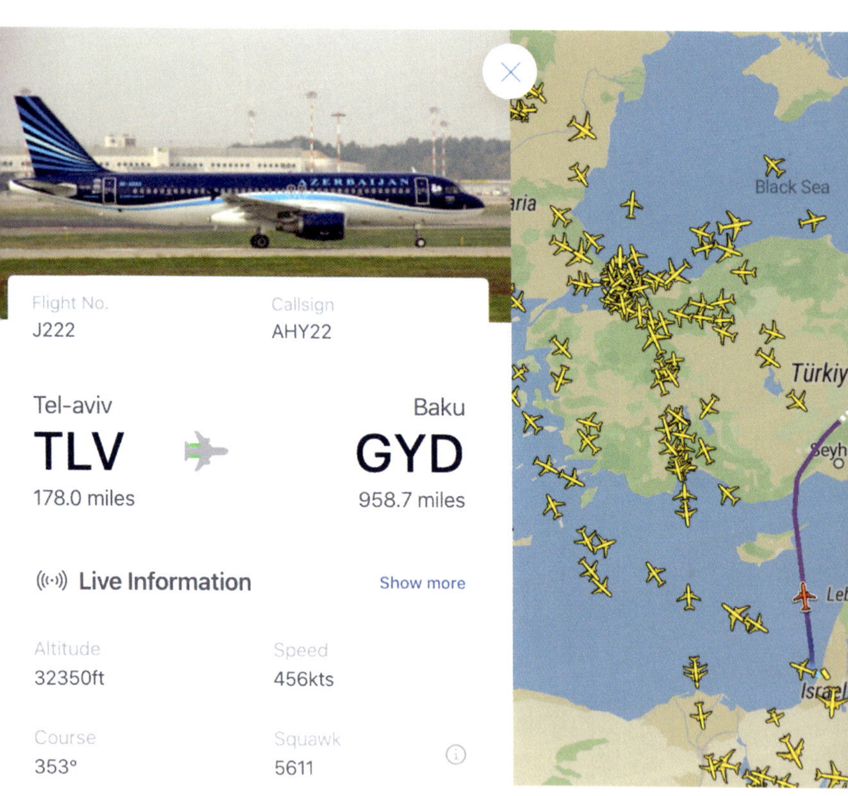
AZERBAIJAN
Flight No.
J222
Callsign
AHY22
Tel-aviv
TLV
178.0 miles
Baku
GYD
958.7 miles
Live Information
Show more
Altitude
32350ft
Speed
456kts
Course
353°
Squawk
5611
Black Sea
Türkiy
Israel

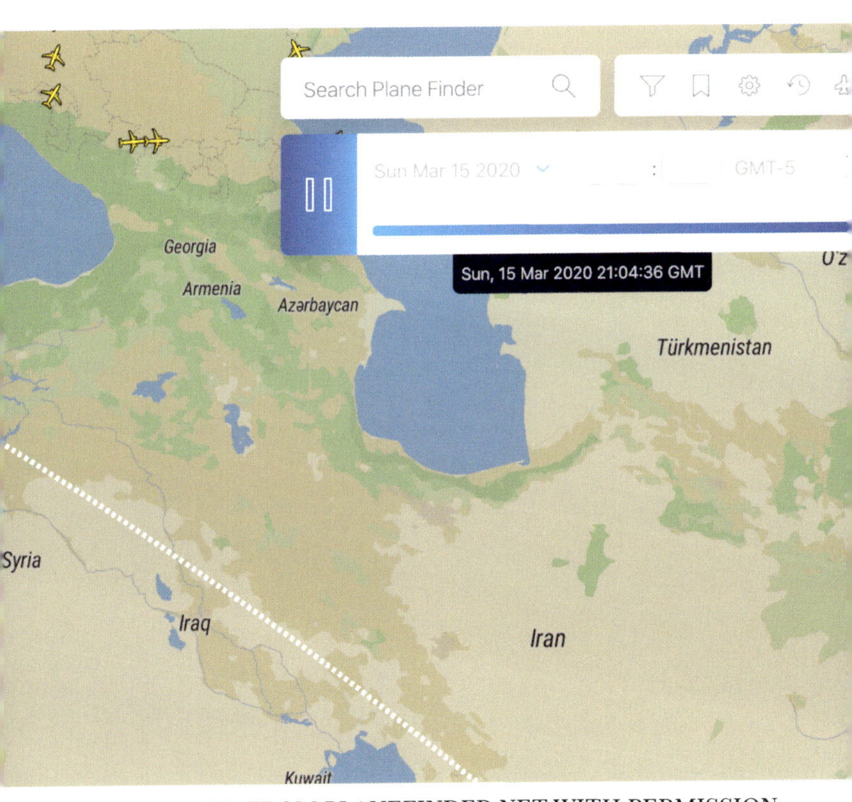

PRINTED FROM PLANEFINDER.NET WITH PERMISSION

FOREWORD

Zoë Matt-Williams

We are making sourdough. I stop my work every twenty minutes, walk to the kitchen and perform the same ritual of stretching and folding the dough eight times. In the evening, we sit in front of our bowl watching bubbles rise, listening to the fizzle as life grows. It takes us three days to make our first loaf.

Around the world people are nurturing their newly conceived sourdough starters—supermarkets log flour shortages and 'How to Bake the Perfect Golden Loaf' articles lurk around every corner. It feels like a bizarre new ritual of mindfulness in a world usually so obsessed with movement and speed.

Much has changed in the past months. We selected these pieces before the virus spread escalated in the UK, and this volume seems to me now a little like a time-capsule, documenting what people were thinking about, writing about, painting about just before. It's full of all sorts of things: a rooftop bath, a goblin-king, a hiding Oyster card, a pair of lime-green crocs, two houseplants wrinkling, hot dogs, dust mites, a head turned motorcycle, a lobster, a guinea pig, a living room fan swirling, loud music in the street—and only one mention of a cigarette, which is really quite impressive for a student publication.

These pieces read differently now than they did when we first selected them. A photograph of a pair of plastic gloves now carries new subtext, just as an image of bodies grouped together resonates in a different way. The pieces that stick out to me most in the way they've changed, however, are the many photos we received of older generations. Looking at them now evokes to me the past weeks' discussions around age, and reminds us of how vulnerability stems not only from the effects of a virus, but from public indifference. We hope reading this anthology now offers us all the chance to think again about who and what we value, and how.

The last months have shown that even a virus is not, as some have argued, a 'great equalizer': lockdown has undeniably impacted some far more than others. Cambridge and Oxford have historically been institutions of immense privilege, and still are. Even outside the context of a pandemic, a publication like the *Mays* occupies a difficult space: it's both a great showcase of new student work and deeply intertwined with the Oxbridge mythology. One of our goals this year was to demystify the *Mays*, and to create a volume that doesn't take itself too seriously, that can be playful just as it can be serious.

Like the snippets of different languages peppering these texts—Spanish, Mandarin, Greek, German, Latin, French, Urdu—our committee members and contributors come not just from the UK, but from around the world. A large part of this anthology has come together via Skype, in bedrooms turned transnational offices. This book is a communal project, and so is reading it. As borders close and countries turn inwards, we return to shared rituals: we read, we write, we sourdough-bake. The pieces in this anthology highlight what ties us together—how we feel our way through the world when we pay attention.

Now more than ever we celebrate the small things, now more than ever we feel in moments. This book is a collection of these moments. Not just the heavy ones, but the light ones, too: like the quiet satisfaction of lying belly-up in the sea.

Thanks to all that helped put together this issue—to the amazing committee who spent hours looking through these submissions and selecting them, sorting through emails, putting up posters—you guys have been the absolute best. Thanks to our contributors, whose pieces have been a joy to read and look at; to Philippe and Oscar, who set aside time for us in both of their very busy lives, and whose input has been absolutely brilliant; to Mark Curtis and Dr Franklin, for all their support along the way; and, of course, to Rebekah, our fabulous deputy editor, invaluable in all of this.

Hope you enjoy. ◆

WEST VIRGINIA, 2019, JOE WILLS

METAMORPHOSES

Olivia Healey

A lobster in a velodrome
Orbiting out in space
A very happy lobster
In a very happy place

An octopus of silver
A triceratops of gold
A mussel of magnesium
Magnificent and cold

The stars above are singing
For the final musketeer
Capellini! Galileo!
Oh gracious goodness—she is here! ◆

SPA DAY

Zehra A.

'Nazia! *Oye,* Nazia!'

Ma'am is calling my name. I glance up at the clock. There is still one minute of my lunch break left. Forty-five seconds. Thirty.

'Nazia! *Tu fire hona chahti heh?*'

Nazia! Do you want to get fired?

Just twenty-five seconds. But I admit defeat. Slip my lunchbox under the bench I am sat on, and walk up to the desk at reception. Straighten my uniform, and smile brightly at the silky-haired woman waiting next to Ma'am. She is a definite category two. I can predict her order before Ma'am recites it, her nasal voice tripping over the English words she claims to know.

'Nazia, Madam wants underarms/legs/underlegs/manicurepedicure/hairmask/ayurvedicMASSAGE!'

Category twos are always the most demanding. This classification system is one that the girls and I came up with years ago, when I first started working at the spa. Category ones are old money, products of Lahore's most cultured homes. They cloak themselves in beige pashminas, wear understated gold hoops, and come to the spa mostly to relax. The heavy-duty stuff they have done at home, by women who have been serving their families for aeons. Head massages with almond oil and bikini waxes are for the bedroom. With us they request their fingernails to be buffed and cut, hair to be washed and trimmed, and fresh face masks to be applied. These women talk on the phone endlessly, uncoupling inappropriate pairings between their sons abroad and the white women they are writing home about, planning elaborate dinners in gilded dining rooms, and generally managing the affairs of their estates. They don't deign to chat with us a great deal, but they appreciate good service. Since many of them have Christian servants at home too, they tip heavily around Christmas and Eastertime. Not easy customers by any means, but almost delightful compared to category twos.

These women—girls—are new money. Some are the products of new textile factories where orange farms used to be, others are the results of unholy alliances between their financier husbands and the Pakistani State Bank. They have a uniform. Bleached hair, designer purses, heavy rocks on their fingers, and sixteen-year-old hired girls who carry their toddlers for them. Category twos are almost feline, unafraid to scratch and shriek if things don't go their way. They pinch their young nannies in public and would probably slap us too, if not for Ma'am's strict policies about the treatment of her staff. And they are competing with everyone. I get sore between my legs just thinking about the number of Hollywoods they pay for each month, but I imagine a hairless vagina is implied in their nuptial agreement. Their English is almost as broken as Ma'am's (even I can see that, comparing them to the category ones), but they work so that you can't tell. After all, there are hundreds of hungry girls like them who didn't get their chance to mate at university. It is sheer determination that got them their current positions. They hate us in particular, because we are a little too close to a life they know about from poorer cousins, the ones they cut off before their weddings took place. Being a category two must be exhausting.

Being a category three, on the other hand, appears to be synonymous with giving precisely zero fucks about your appearance. We added this last category after we had all encountered these hairy young women with glasses pushed up their noses, who flinch awkwardly at every wax strip. Category threes are *bahir ki larkian*. Girls from abroad. These girls have left Pakistan to pursue their education in Amreeka, Englistan, and other Western countries that appear in the dramas we all watch at home. They speak heavily accented Urdu, and appear to be perpetually embarrassed by what is going on. Once a year a whole group of them comes to invite us to the *Aurat March*, the Women's March that they organise on the streets of Lahore. Last year I told them that I couldn't afford to miss a day's wages for the hypothetical promise that my future husband wouldn't beat me in the years to come, and they grew frenzied, their eyes welling with tears. They promised me that they would march for me, and forgot to tip on their way out.

▪

But this woman has no such pretensions to female empowerment. She wants to be dealt with fast, so that she can host her sister's engagement party with a glabrate glow. I lead her up to the white-walled room, and start to heat up some fruit wax. Uncharacteristically for her type, she appears to be taking a break from typing furiously on a phone the size of a small TV screen. I test the waters, see if she wants to talk instead.

'*Baji*, you prefer me to do waxing first? Not manipedi?'

She glances up at me, as if only now realising that I can speak.

'Yes, what else? You want me to mess up my nails while getting waxed? Do they not train you here?'

Best not to talk, then.

I finish her waxing in silence, save for the sound of the strips slapping between her thighs, once, twice, thrice for the most stubborn ingrown hairs. I think about one of the category threes who once glanced up from a book she had brought with her to ask me whether I get embarrassed or uncomfortable touching sweaty, naked women all day. I thought about my answer carefully before I answered. Women who have been living abroad may generally be more liberal, but that does not mean they want to hear the truth. So I told her a half-lie. I don't mind the work because I treat it as work, and at least the environment is clean, and all the men are gay, so there is no fear of harassment. This is part of the truth, so this is what I told her. I withheld that sometimes, on my sensitive days, I do mind the set-up. I mind being inches away from the stale, tangled armpit hair of a woman who has not bothered to ask my name. I mind being told endless stories about talented children who are learning Angrezi (English) *so fast*, and knowing that if I talk about my own little Primrose, I will be reported for audacious chatting. And I mind the way they laugh when they ask about *your Christmas*. Their Eid is my Eid. So why is my Christmas not theirs, too?

■

After we are done with the waxing, I lead the woman over to the pedicure station. This is my favourite part of the job. The room is warmly lit, and there are candles glowing on the windowsill. She relaxes into the plush chair, and I bring a basin for her treatment. I begin to massage her feet in warm water, pressing my fingers in so that my knuckles align with her toes. I once had a customer start moaning while I did this, and myself and all the other girls stifled our laughter until she had left, then laughed ourselves silly in the break room.

For days after, someone had only to say, 'She must *really* not get any at home!' and we would all set off again.

But back to my woman. I bring over the nail varnish selection to her, predicting in my head that she will choose a turquoise blue. The colour is all the rage in Pakistani designer circles right now (I would know, since they all get their eyebrows threaded here), and she will want to match her outfit. Surprisingly, she goes for a baby pink. As I take it out of the box, she tells me that her eye-makeup will be pink, so she wants to match it. I forgot that make-up has to be factored into the look, too—not just outfit choice.

Presently, her phone dies. She begins talking to me, a monologue of sorts. The topic is her little genius of a son, who is learning English fast and becoming a regular 'Shack-spare' (whoever that is). He is also taking a fast-track French course ahead of a holiday they are taking at the end of the summer.

I ask out of genuine curiosity: 'Madam, can he speak Urdu?'

She laughs for the first time. 'No! Thank God, his Urdu is as poor as can be. English is the language of the future, has no one told you?'

I think about Primrose at home, and how I was discussing this very topic with her over dinner last night. I was telling her how all these rich kids speak English, not Punjabi, Urdu and Saraiki like her. She must learn, and work at her studies, so that she can succeed in life. I tell all this to the woman while I file her toenails, since she has opened up to me.

Then I tell her how Primrose's eyes had widened, and how she asked me very seriously: 'Amma, do these kids not know any language apart from English and a little Urdu?'

I replied: 'Yes, *beta,* that is what I am telling you.'

'*Haye*! *Becharay*!'

Oh! The poor things!

I feel the woman stiffen, and know I have misspoken. She digs her heels into the basin, demands that I hurry up and stop talking nonsense. I finish the rest of her treatment without saying another word, hurriedly applying the plasticky-pink varnish. On her way out, she remarks to Ma'am that some of her girls are getting particularly cocky. She fails to leave a tip. ◆

DOLCE MAMA, SOLAL BAUER

TARTE AUX FRAMBOISES

Katharina Friege

There is something beautiful
in the man who came in from the rain
and the mud
and saw the tarte aux framboises
and cut it carefully into eighths—
a wheel of fortune
a pizza
a metaphor
(balancing precariously on this illusion or the other)
a gift or
a promise with no beginning, no end
a mathematics equation in the third grade.

Did you see how he
brushed the crumbs off the edge of the knife
and placed it in the sink
and took from the cupboard between square fingers
a dainty painted porcelain cup

and a dainty painted porcelain saucer
and another, and another—
and brewed the tea
and poured the milk
and passed the sugar
and shared the tarte
one bite after the other? ◆

OFFSHORE CHOREOGRAPHIES, MARIA KAMINSKA

SHORELINES

Alejandro Lemus-Gomez

A beastly green arthritic mountain range backdrops
Bisabuelo Augusto, his legs spread on sand,
pant legs rolled up on khaki calves with toes wriggling
in the tawny tropical beach like minnows,
what a shame que no tienes sus ojos claros, mother says
looking at my earthen almond eyes remembering
Augusto's aquamarine gaze dazzling like Oriente shores
yearning for the Atlantic, the hustle of Havana
to the west, to cut a palm tree, to fashion a raft, and drift
with thick, verdant fronds for sails
and his shovel—dirty from farm work—as a paddle,
with each stroke bits of mountain's grit
breadcrumbing his journey to America, land of English,
housing bubbles, and hot dogs
that my mother would eat when reaching New York
escaping Cuba, Castro, and Soviet entropy

for a greasy taste of freedom, a pair of navy-blue Ralph Lauren sneakers,
a son not forced to wear pionero red,
and the shores of Georgian lakes, she and I wading in muddy water
dodging driftwood, her reflections on each wave,
what a shame he never saw esos ojos de tierra pura,
de café in the morning, sipping liberty, cream and sugar. ◆

HASHIM

Eli Nelson

This is what you said
to me: the moon was white
around my head. I replied
that light and dark were swimming
on my eyes. A voice,
you said, was moving down your spine.
I said I saw two beasts,
a peacock: his blaze of feather shimmered
in your face of countless colours. The other
was a mountain-lion.
You told me that the fountains
in my eyes had overflowed.
Some spirit, as it moves
leaves residue ◆

FULL SPEED (CRISS-CROSS), YUL HR KANG

Solal Bauer

CHAMPAGNE, TREVOR

We're going to a club with the guys from the play about choir boys sleeping together.

I thought the play was trying too hard to be scandalous when I saw it last week, but tonight, I think it's 'a daring look under the veil of one of this country's most secretive institutions, a breath-taking demand that queer people be seen and heard—5 stars'. Really, it's an excuse to put some boys in shorts; Stan has 'forgotten' to change out of his costume, and will continue to forget all night.

We're being led by the big two: Trevor and Claude. They choose who's in and who's out, and right now I'm in. I owe them everything I've got here. Trevor edits one of the big papers temporarily, though he can't write—none of the reviewers here can. Claude wrote the play about choir boys in shorts kissing choir boys in shorts, which makes him a big deal.

I've had my lanyard for 3 days now. I nicked a VIP card from one of the offices, which means I've got an extra one to give out. It's nice to be powerful. It's easy too—here, all I have to do is give Trevor the odd hug, write that a show was a 'ramshackle smorgasbord of conflicting styles' twice a week, and make sure not to sleep with anyone.

I try to walk with Claude, whose online dating profile is filthier than the bottom streets of this wrinkled-up double-decker city. The others call him Mother, which makes sense.

‘Did you hear about *Angels in America* getting cancelled?’ I ask.

‘Yeah, dreadful.’

‘Do you… do you think they’ll keep performing it?’

There’s a silence, and then he laughs at me for a long time. ‘You’ve really done it now,’ he says. I try to laugh too. Claude is bald. I struggle with Claude.

I overhear Trevor talking about me, and he calls me ‘my boy’.

I’m walking with Phoebe now, who just now on the terrace confessed that she broke up with her last boyfriend because he ‘wouldn’t take it’. I let out a delighted scream when she told me. Tonight, she’s going for Stan, but she’s far too confident around him so I’m not counting on it. I think that for someone like Stan, there must be something quite terrifying about a woman who actually wants to fuck you.

We catch up to the boys, an indeterminate gaggle of tight jawlines and slicked back blonde hair, and they follow Stan down into this opening in the ground. Our faces go bright red in the light, we flash our lanyards for a hit of precious dopamine without looking at the bouncer, and we’re in.

Last week, Trevor took me to this private rooftop bar with a view of all seven of the city’s hills. He told me that nobody at the festival exists. They look so shiny on this immersive stage, but when you reach out to touch them, your hand goes straight through. They rise out of the earth for these three weeks, float about, and then crumble. They shed their scaly worldly skin in exchange for a seductive, fleetingly hedonistic glance at what their lives might have been like if only they weren't so boring. Trevor's popular, but he's easy to take advantage of. He wields his expiring influence the way people who've made it big too fast spend their money: extravagantly, carelessly, tastelessly. He's got the Gucci logo belt equivalent of a social life, chatting up D-list celebrities and rising actors and cementing his friendships with swipes of the company credit card he's allowed so little time with. He's got this inquisitive look about him that makes him appear all infantile and loveable, but naive as well, completely out of his depth. He hasn't got a chin. He tells me I'm the only real person he's met here, and I blow him a kiss. Later that week, Adela would watch me sit on Trevor's lap and drill into him with my blue eyes in exchange for a bottle of champagne. 'I read your article yesterday, thought it was really well written, I'm trying to get my hands on some tickets for Ed Knowles but I'm short on cash.' She'd call me a sycophant, say she'd rather pay for her own drinks, and I'd be embarrassed and tell her it's all power games, it's not real. She doesn't really understand. She feels sorry for Trevor because he can't tell we're all pretending, but I think he knows. He must know, surely.

As we stroll into the middle of the bar, I catch Phoebe biting Stan's earlobe. Phoebe isn't real either—like all of us, she's only really alive in this shiny world, grasping at power she doesn't have. Our bodies are screens onto which the festival projects heightened versions of ourselves. And yet, later, when Claude shouts 'that's an ass' and gives Stan's a slap, the images glitch for a moment. I ask Stan if he's alright. He tells me he's the only one of his classmates to have been cast straight out of drama school. It's whatever, we let it slide, we're not ready for that conversation anyway. I take his hand in mine.

'I love how rough and manly your hands feel.'

It's eczema.

Trevor's credit card gets us champagne. I'm at a table with some comedians I know from TV now. I'm putting on an American accent. We request Madonna but they never put her on. I'm calling too many people 'bitch'. I'm half as old as anyone else here. Somebody's going to send me a bobblehead of themselves in the mail. We're comparing lanyards like we're in *American Psycho*. Ryan says his 50-year-old boyfriend has transferred him a small fortune. I don't think Ryan has a boyfriend. The lead from *Angels in America* has his leg in a cast. I give my spare VIP card to a stranger in exchange for a sticker. A woman tells me she's like a lesbian Ellen Page. Stan tells Phoebe he's not interested. Knew it.

I'm a star.

I follow Phoebe and the choir boys behind a curtain under the stairs where they keep the speakers. The music here is fucking deafening, and the space is tiny. We dance through the hearing damage, it's totally euphoric and I forget I'm not in the play, and Phoebe's getting close to me, and she pushes me onto the floor at the back of the cupboard and kisses me exactly the way I'd expect her to, which is far too passionately, and the boys are trying not to fall on us, and I ask myself how it feels, and it feels like I'm sticking my tongue through a raw chicken wing whilst trying not to die. I open my eyes to Claude pushing the curtain aside and winking at me, so I show him my teeth. Phoebe whispers in my ear 'I'm going to fuck you' and I say 'No you're not' and she says louder 'I am. Yes I am' so I put both my hands on her shoulders and look at her until she realises. 'Oh, you don't feel anything?' I tell her I don't, and she asks me 'Really? Nothing?' and kisses me again, and I say 'I swear' and she says 'Shit' and I say 'It's like sticking my tongue through a raw chicken wing' though at this point she can't hear me over the music.

She pulls me up the stairs to the smoking area where we kiss for another half an hour on a battered picnic table. We laugh because the people up here must think it's real. 'This is all a performance, right?' 'Yeah, one hundred percent.' I wrap my legs around her waist and kiss her more. 5 stars, a tour de force.

Claude told me there's people here who can end a career with a sentence. Imagine.

We come back downstairs and I lose Phoebe almost instantly. I'm alone now, trying not to look lost, but the bar is far more crowded than I remember and it feels like I'm an ant pushing through gelatine. Suddenly Trevor grabs me from behind, pulls me in and hugs me with his mouth against my ear, and somehow I can smell his breath. He's trying to string a sentence together but he can't, and all that's coming out is this warped garble, so I push my way out of his grip, turn around, and consider his face with a kind of academic fascination—his somersaulting eyes, their dilated pupils, his mouth melting down onto his chest without a chin to get in its way. I picture a line of choir boys staring straight ahead, hypnotised, the skin on their faces peeling back as thousands of bloody worms erupt from their eyes and mouths. Trevor goes for a kiss and misses, landing instead on my shoulder where he mumbles Friends? You're my friend, and automatically

I say yeah, Trevor, sure I am, and over his shoulder I catch sight of Claude doing a line with one of the blond boys still wearing his uniform and I think, 'What in the world am I doing here?'

As the festival nears its end, we're all dead, or dying, or about to die. In a week, none of these people will exist, myself included. I could get a coffee with Trevor in London, and it'll be Trevor's face and ginger hair, but he'll be Trevor the waiter at Bartelli's, nothing like the suited-up big-shot editor I've gotten to know here. Might as well give him a different name. Claude will go back to being retired. He'll travel to see Stan on his European tour, multiple times I presume, and maybe Stan will recognise him in the audience. Phoebe? I really couldn't tell you.

Trevor is vegetating on one of the sofas. I leave the bar and as I walk home through the gothic streets, I drink in the cold sinister splendour of this city folded back on itself. I find Phoebe sobbing, waiting to cross the road under a lonely streetlight, and I give her a hug so we don't have to talk. 'Sleepover?' she begs. Fuck it, why not? She leads me down a steep alleyway to the foggy under-city, past imposing stone arches and neon club signs until we reach a small green door recessed into the brick. As we make our way up the dim stairwell with its peeling yellow paint, I realise that I'm fucking terrified of this woman. Witless.

This is where I die, I know it. Who the hell invites people they're not going to sleep with back to their room? She unlocks the door and, before opening it, looks back at me with a mischievous, hungry leer. I finger the Victorinox in my back jeans pocket and flip open the blade, just in case. She leads me into her room, we get into bed fully clothed, and she's finally going to pin me down and stab my eyes and slit my throat in some kind of insane ritual murder sex frenzy, I'm so ready for it, but instead she dozes off with tears still drying on her face, her lipstick leaving bloody gashes across her pillow.

I wait. I'm sure she's fast asleep. I creep out of bed, cut off a strand of her hair, let myself out, and wander away, a dark mass against the glistening cobblestones. ◆

BREAK, ISAAC ZAMET

THE SUCCULENT

E. L. Hallesy

When, every other week,
I am back with you, I water it
because you forget.

Green-apple flesh begs
for rain, each springy leaf tip
shyly rouged, angled

to the light. In the glass jar's
pebble base, water clots the soil
into mud, pooling darkly.

We bought it young, now,
slowly, it outgrows the brim,
rubbing up against the glass.

I let my fingertip slide,
halting, in rubbery staccato
down the leaf's grip, plying

its juicy spring.

But I come back to find the leaves
soft, one deep wrinkle

banking the midrib.
(I google: when healthy the plant
is fleshy and thickened,

adapted for drought, the roots
store moisture for weeks in the sap,
Latin: *sucus* (juice).

The succulent, unlike
other plants, opens its stomata
only at night.

It is hard to tell the signs
of too much, or too little, water
from lack of natural light.)

Translucent drop-leaves callus,
flesh-coloured on the soil, dying. When
is it enough?

At night in my bath,
without you, in the desert of midweek
I turn off the gasping

fan, lock the door and let steam
jungle the air til it is so thick
I can barely see,

and mist, sated
on the cold wall, drips a path
down the paintwork.

I sink and open my eyes
and mouth beneath the bath's supple skin,
let my thighs

drift, wet flesh buoyant. I see
the troubled surface suffer
a thousand local crises

in its poise. Fluid
sound is swollen and I hear my bones
crack and liquefy until

I am all water,
and I think of it there by the windowpane,
parched and waiting. ◆

ELYSIAN

Sona Popat

crawler of oceans, chloroplasts
curled unto, appropriated, stolen, swallowed
whole and kept—

like cronus unhinged
his jaw and took zeus into his mouth:
a protection and a use and a stolen
good.

pandora here examines the box, sees
pod protrusion and
oxygen bubbles rising and
the iridescent curl of skin, swaying just to
in the tide. she says:
well here! this just doesn't make any sense.
and—

though it's difficult to digest, a failing
classification system propagating—

oxygen bubbles rise.
cohesion spits
hollows in the ocean and,
basking in the sun,
E. chlorotica grows. ◆

TAPESTRY OF HOME, POL BRADFORD-CORRIS

ANTHROPOCENE DIARIES: JANUARY 2020

Georgie Newson-Errey

You stand on the cliff's edge, staring down at a mass of agitated grey froth. You know that it reminds you of something, but can't figure out what.

Mouthchurned toothpaste? Almost, but not quite. It's that *texture*: grainy, unbroken, furrowed, glitching... you realise that what you are remembering is the texture of water as it appears on Google Earth. You remember the hours you spent as a kid zooming in endlessly on Google's oceans, watching the pixels scramble and shift, drilling further and further until the screen was a single shade of dull blue. You remember the shiny satisfaction of having completed a game, proven a point, exhausted an omnipotence.

▪

The darkness of your childhood bedroom is a special kind of darkness, clotted with spectres and longing. Now, the darkness holds a small rectangle of light, and the rectangle holds Australia, which is burning. Someone has posted a photo of a vast cloud of smoke engulfing a town; you use your thumb and index finger to zoom in on it.

The cloud is an inside with no outsides, thick with soot and soundlessness. A hardboiled gloam-light tinges it a delicate orange, the colour of a whisked egg, but its troughs and vortices are darker, wilder. A network of fields and houses sits placidly in the foreground, as neatly delineated as a circuit board. Above them, the loose stuffing of a dead planet ruptures through the sky.

Your Dad manages to get in touch with his siblings. Your uncle's farm has been hit hard by the blaze, so he's gone to stay with his kids. He's okay. Just reeling from the shock.

Three weeks later, you will see the photograph again, this time as a meme. The image quality will have decreased from the soft trauma of endless circulation, so the cloud will look solid and brittle and grubby. The houses will be labelled 'Society in 2011' and the cloud will be labelled 'Party Rock Anthem – LMFAO'. It will be, for a brief while, the funniest thing you have ever seen.

▪

In the backlit cases of the new natural history museum, which is clean and hushed and bubblegum-smelling, neat little signs have been propped up next to each dead thing. The signs are circular and colour-coded, like board game counters, and they tell you the 'extinction rating' of the species to which the dead thing in question belongs. Green means not currently threatened. Red means existentially endangered. Most of the signs are yellow and orange. If you step back from the cases and half-close your eyes the signs look quite pretty, reassuringly plastic amidst all that startled fur, but if you come too close and think too hard they become terrible things, garish and smirking, and your chest fills up with sour air and your right leg starts to quiver and you want to scrunch up your eyes for a long time and not look at the dead things or their stupid signs ever again. So you walk away and your breathing steadies and, after a while, you forget. But then, later, when you are admiring a fossil of a plesiosaur, maybe, or the glazed shinbone of a triceratops (both of which are such decidedly dead dead things that their 'extinction rating' is too total to be relevant; a colour beyond red), they reappear, the signs, swimming hazily in your vision like the memory of hurt, and you imagine it, of course you imagine it how could you not imagine it—a human person, cased in glass, skin stuffed, limbs twisted, eyes blackbeaded and mournful, and the sign, the sign gentleblinking as if made of something electric and terrible, fluttering and beckoning and changing, hesitantly, like a distant traffic light, from green to red.

▪

You feel guilty all the time. You feel guilty for eating. You feel guilty for not eating. You feel guilty for writing. You feel guilty for not writing. You feel guilty for being unproductive. You feel guilty for having internalised a neoliberal ideal of permanent hyper-productivity. You feel guilty for being privileged. You feel guilty for feeling guilty about being privileged, when really you should just be feeling lucky, and then, like, devoting your life to A Cause, or at least studying medicine or something.

The guilt is like an itch that cannot be scratched, an itch somewhere deep in the sweetsour tubing of your gut. The guilt is like a fine, irritating dust that settles into your ribcage and slowly crystallises into a glaring diamond. The guilt makes you think Bad Things, sometimes, because the Bad Things tell you that you're being silly, that you haven't had it so easy, that you're special, that the things making you feel ashamed are the real problem, that you can—for a short while—feel deliciously, blisteringly numb to the guilt.

You feel really, really guilty for thinking the Bad Things.

▪

There is an insect trapped in the bathwater. You don't know if it is desperately struggling or just being battered around by the current beneath the running tap. You hope that it is dead, so that what looks like frantic resistance is in fact absolute submission. But when you reach in and gently scoop it up with your palm, you realise that it is not an insect at all: simply a small clod of black fluff.

▪

Something is shifting; you can hear it everywhere. It is in the voices on the news and the faces on the train and the hot mouths of the bustling crowd. It is in the spluttering of the engine and wink of the camera and hum of the laptop. Sometimes it speaks to you and you only, and sometimes its speech is in words. The words are always the same. They pulse through you in a single beat, both expunged and received, momentary and non-cognitive, like a sneeze or an *Iloveyou*. They come to you as you walk around a supermarket, gazing at the Tetris-rows of saccharine abundance. They come to you as you watch a man in a gown step over a sleeping body, the metronomic tap-tap of his dress shoes momentarily fractured but swiftly resumed. They come to you as you look out over a flooded riverbank with the person you love, clutching hands so tightly that you leave half-moon imprints in one another's knuckles.

This can't last this can't last this can't last this can't last this can't last this can't

■

The snowdrops come out early. You've suspected for a while now that apocalypse is always—subtly, grotesquely, for a short while, for the lucky ones—a tiny bit beautiful.

■

The pub is usually full of theatregoers, but tonight there's a different crowd. One of the men who pushes past you is wearing a thinning patchwork jacket emblazoned with a battered, palpably dirty Union Jack. A too-obvious metaphor, if you believe in it, which he doesn't. The man's friends make up about half the congregation; the other half is comprised of a group of boys in suits. A drinking society, maybe, or some sort of club. They've got to be students, but it's difficult to tell how old they are; they all seem polished, shiny, faceless, like toy soldiers.

When the clock strikes midnight there is cheering and stamping and singing, like at New Year's. The boys in suits do not join in with the festivities, but they throw a few approving smirks in the general direction. You move within earshot of their conversation, wondering if they will be discussing the only thing there is to discuss.

Oh, no, San Fran's horrible now, one of the boys is saying. Stifling, and full of homeless. His cigarette glows bloodily in the soft, alkaline dark.

▪

An Instagram post informs you that fireflies are dying out. You scroll past it quickly, so that it doesn't have the chance to become real. Out of the window, far in the distance, you can see headlights in motion: tight twists of brightness pulled slowly across a black screen. ◆

SUMMONING, EMILY ▸

WHITE PAWN, F2

Ben Aroya Philipps

Thus beggares and barones at debat aren ofte.
— LANGLAND

And the pawn—whose small step
is catastrophe writ large—creeps unsurely
from dark to light, from nothing
to action. Threatens the black bishop,
quakes at the queen: is ignored
by both. Some small function in some
small reptilian brain tells the pawn
that this is the wrong move.
This move is wrong because it
ends the game too early; this move
is wrong because
it ends the game with no flourish,
without the pounding of big feet. ◆

A BEND OR

Ben Aroya Philipps

[*Scrope v Grosvenor* (1389) *was one of the earliest heraldic law cases brought in England, caused by two of King Richard II's knights realising they had the same coat of arms. Among the several hundred witnesses heard during the four-year case were Owain Glyndŵr, the Welsh rebel prince, and Geoffrey Chaucer.*]

Inside the storm of whirling vanity the Welshman sits
and thinks of his forebears. Madog and ancient Blethyn
pageant unseen across the church where magnates bicker,
feud, and invoke the Saxons, and through it all he sits
upright, hands on knees, glaring forward and waiting
to speak. Two rows behind and to the left, another stares
bored at dust-mites swirling in a beam of light
dividing the floor. He thinks of his creations;
the obscene wife, the prostrate, howling lover, the mother
tongue. And still the litigants point and shriek, at
the front, getting nowhere—until a new witness is called
and the weary bodies draped across the pews in vain
readjust, peering down the aisle to where
wealth and rank spar with blunted swords. The prince
and the poet tap their feet on the cold stone floor. ◆

CARRY IT

Daniya Baiguzhayeva

Say an albatross dies mid-flight
drops down miles its compact
missile of flesh cutting through
sheets of air its wings torsioned
together by impossible velocities
till it lands wreathed around the
neck of a small child so small it
is stooping under the weight of
it this heavy just-alive bird the
child speechless with fear walks
around gesturing first up at the
sky then at the bird its cruel un
-ceasing geotropism and all the
adults say the same things like
start 'em off young! and *I'll bet it's*
a fad and you'll grow you'll grow
into that. ◆

A PIVITOL SPACE, CHARLOTTE BIRD

THE SUN, OUR IMPERMANENT STAR

Imani Thompson

Tower Hill. A day that moves too slowly despite one being late for everything. She has forgotten to touch up her lipstick and is wearing a long green coat with deep pockets (the sort things get lost in). She is looking for her Oyster card. Her little girl is beside her. Rosie is six and insists on wearing odd socks and twirling whenever she enters a shop. Her mum can't always work her out; but she loves her more than she ever thought it possible to love.

Her phone rings.

'Hi love.' She takes Rosie's hand.

'Hey babe, what time do you think you'll be back?' It is her husband.

'We're just getting on the tube now, around five?' She has found her Oyster card.

'Cool.'

There is something in Kai's voice.

'Why are you asking?'

'I've asked Sophie to come babysit tonight. Rosie will be okay with that, won't she?'

'Why?'

'It's a surprise.'

She blushes. 'Rosie, are you okay with Sophie looking after you tonight?'

'Sophie!' Rosie jumps.

'I think she prefers Sophie to us,' she says.

'Great. I'll see you later. Love you.'

'Love you too.'

'Love you more.'

The blush deepens. 'Come on, missie.'

Rosie takes her mum's hand as they go through the barriers.

'Mummy, can Sophie and me watch Swan Lake?'

'But you made her watch that with you last time, and the time before.'

'Please, it's our favourite.'

She is not paying too much attention to her daughter, for she is looking at the advertisements down the escalator. She is looking out for … there it is: the poster advertising the collection she helped curate at the *V&A*. Tom Winston's photography. '*Clocks and memories of Grandma. The boy started his career by taking pictures in the garden.*' It has been so long, she thinks, since she's sat in the garden and—

'Mummy, if you were to turn into a swan do you think it would be painful or feel nice?'

'That's hard to say. What do you think?' She has to pull Rosie out of the way of a woman ignoring everything but her phone call. They come to the platform. 'I think it might hurt at the beginning and then be nice.'

Any unattended items will be—

‘Rosie, don’t touch that.’

‘But it’s pretty.’

‘It’s on the floor.’

The Circle and District. Yellow and green; green and yellow. Rosie is now talking about the boys and girls in her class, who is kissing who. Her mum is trying to remember if she kissed anyone so young. She is also admiring the shoes of the woman beside her; deciding that she will cut her hair; remembering to call her father.

The train arrives. A man and his dog get off as Rosie and her mum get on. She gives Rosie the seat that’s left.

The next station is Liverpool Street. Please mind the gap—

A man takes a half run and jumps, just making it. Someone smiles at him. He is tall, wearing a grey suit. A suit which— She looks at him. And

five years of her life,

and just

maybe, the entirety of the sun, rush behind him and are trapped by the now-closed doors.

‘Emily,’ he says.

■

‘Emily. Emily?’

‘Yes?’ She comes out from the bathroom wearing a black slip, a toothbrush in her hand.

Kai sits on the edge of the bed. ‘Are you okay?’

He is not wearing a shirt, and Emily thinks how her husband is beautiful. *My husband is beautiful.*

'Did you not like the restaurant?' His voice stiff. 'I wanted to treat you, thought it would be… what's going on?'

'I'm sorry. It's just been one of those days, I…' She turns back into the bathroom, rinses her toothbrush.

He follows her. 'Talk to me. No more silence.'

She catches sight of her face in the mirror, knows that she is about to cry. *My husband is beautiful.* 'I saw a man get hit by a car today. I think he died.'

She has never lied like that.

She cries.

'Fuck, sweetheart. Come here. Here.' Her husband is kind and will ask no more questions.

She lets herself lean into him.

▪

She does not like her hair shorter; she cannot decide which way to part it. She cannot decide if she thinks this day is too hot or too cold. She cannot decide… *Knock*.

'You came.' He is startled and pleased.

'You won't tell anyone?'

'If that's what you want.'

'It is.'

'Then I won't.'

There is a shudder in the air.

'Can I come in?'

He steps aside for her.

'It's like we're having an affair.' He smiles as she moves further into the bright hallway.

'What?' She is distracted by the Matisse: a print of his two dancers. 'It's the one I… you still have it after all these years.'

Both are now staring at the picture.

'It hasn't been that many years, has it?'

It is not, she realises, the air shuddering, but herself.

Sun crashing into concrete.

'Can I get you a drink?' He moves past her.

'Yes please.' She follows him into the kitchen. A large space, the flat must have been expensive.

'Do you rent or…' She looks at a chair she would never have let him buy.

'I bought it a couple of years ago.'

'I'm glad work is going well.' She re-parts her hair.

'My job's my life I guess. So nothing to spend all the money on.' He laughs.

She thinks she might fall over for the pain that shoots her stomach.

'I have coffee, tea, um something stronger?' His movements jitter.

'Got any vodka?'

'Do you still drink it neat?'

'I never quite grew up.'

Him fixing the drinks, she walks to the window; watches the cars below her; watches the clouds.

Soon he is beside her holding two glasses. They each take a sip. He grimaces; she smiles.

'You still look… the same,' he says.

'Hardly.'

'You do. You—' He stops himself.

'I look tired,' she says, and drinks.

Both at the window. Both watching the cars then the clouds.

'Are we starting this?' He doesn't look at her.

She takes a moment. 'I don't know. I don't think so. It's hard what with… it's hard. After seeing you, I just so wanted to see you again. I hope you don't mind.'

'No. I'm glad that you came. How long has it been?'

'Seven years. We last saw each other at your father's—'

'I remember.' He has moved away from her.

She begins to walk around the space, looking at things, saying things which mean nothing. He sits on the sofa, his eyes following her. She finishes her drink; he doesn't.

Eventually she stops talking and is before him. He stands, cups her chin—she thinks how his hands are the same—they kiss.

■

Later, an absolute silence to the air; neither dare move. Then, wind under his blinds. For how many seconds can they count seconds? His nakedness makes her think that this is the first time anything has ever been. Her nakedness makes him think of oceans and Bob Dylan (it always has).

Thousands of seconds, then thousands more collect about them.

'Where did you go for those years?' she asks, their palms touching.

'South America. Is your sister still a cow?'

She laughs. 'Yes. Is your back still giving you problems?'

'Yes.'

'I saw Rob the other day.'

'Really, how is he?'

'Good. Married now.'

Their palms, chests and fingers touching.

'What's your husband called?'

'How do you know I'm married?'

'You're wearing a wedding ring, Em.'

Now just fingers touching.

'Kai.'

'Did you tell Kai about me?'

'Yes.'

'Did you tell him about—'

'Yes.'

'You have a little girl?'

'I do. I thought it would be too late to have another child but… I do.'

Emily knows that he will cry.

She closes her eyes.

▪

The air colder now, the afternoon flattening.

'It's a great restaurant. I went the weekend it opened. With some girlfriends.' Emily is in front of the bed, re-dressing. She both knows and no longer knows her body.

'Friends I know?'

'No, new friends. The food was great, the cocktails were better.'

'I'll have to check it out with my new friends.' He's leaning against the headboard. 'Argentinian, isn't it?'

'That's right. You must have learnt some recipes, being in South America so long?'

'Only how to barbecue half a cow.' He moves to sit at the edge of the bed.

She laughs, has buttoned her shirt up wrong and has to re-button it.

'I could make you dinner if you like?' he says. 'I might just be a little while walking around London looking for a cow.'

'We could call up my sister.'

How his eyes glint when he laughs. A wicked and perfect laugh. She is dressed but for her shoes.

'Or I could cook us something else? Order something in?'

'It's… I… time,' she says.

Holding her gaze. 'It doesn't have to be.' He stands abruptly.

She steps back. 'I'm married now. I'm married and you know we can't. This, it's just one afternoon… a whole life… another… we tried. We tried that.'

'Did we?' He steps away.

Pressed to the wall. 'Don't….I've never, for one day, not thought of Noah. And you. I dream of him all the time. Sometimes when I walk the streets and the air is too hot I feel his… Noah's…'

'His hand, yeah? Holding yours, or a kid laughs and for a moment it's him. Fall asleep at my desk and he's… Every house with a garden could be ours with him. Every street corner… When I saw you on the train I thought, there, there, her, you—let me have them back.'

She is away from him now, in the sitting room looking for her shoes. There is panic.

'You still don't say his name.' There is anger.

'What?'

'Noah. His name. You still don't... why the fuck not?'

'Don't start this again.'

'No you're right, none of it matters.' The shoes cannot be found.

'Don't leave.' There is fear.

'Of course I have to leave.'

The anger catches and blisters before she is awash with tears. It is over.

He is beside her, holding her.

they soften

It is over,

she repeats.

▪

By the time she is in the hallway the light has dimmed. He has given her a photograph of that time; she has said they will send one email each summer.

That which was, now coming to (an afternoon, a half breath of time, love), all slipped into her pocket; all fumbled within her fingers as she puts on her coat and does up its buttons. By the door now. He still in his dressing gown, undone. He still, in the hallway,

standing beside a piece of sunlight. ◆

UNTITLED #1, GROZ

BATHSHEBA REPLIES

Isabella Fox

Yes, I did bathe on the roof
That night, as was my custom in the evening.
My husband was fighting in the great war outside the city
And the sky was the colour of perfume.

There was the whole world of sky and stone to gaze upon
But the King chose me. I loved my husband
As one loves a golden collar or the redness of
pomegranate seeds.
His love was richer than wine.

The verses they wrote about me gave me no words
As though I followed silent to the steps of the palace
And stood quiet before the King
And lay voiceless beneath him.

But my husband died, and the King's baby in me died.
And David came so quickly. I don't think my hair had
even dried. ◆

小白

Rebecka Nordenlöw

This outing to Seaford will be a first time
with you. Let's trace the Cretaceous layers,
like I did the angles of your hip bones,
lapped by dark waters in a black-and-white
world-view with no room for overlay.
Yet, in Eastern thought that isn't a fault
but a productive union in kind—
while antithetical? So I agree
that we shall share these first-lasts together.
Though you don't seem to compute and never
recognise all shades of grey: of cocc-
olithophores, cephalopods.
These marks are the fossils of my accusation
Because you would never come out in China ◆

AMMAN, MAISS RAZEM

WILLOW MELLOW-WELLOW WONDER

Marnie Shutter

Could you, could you, I mean really,
could you imagine the
path of the lascivious, horn-tailed
goblin king—strapped to the
destiny of a river-cat,
gliding down the aisle of
blurred, sugary milk,
lapping it all up in wonder.

Would you, would you, I mean really,
would you do what he did last Friday,
down by the toucan's upturned
bravado-laced smirk (mercury
freckles);
dancing like a widower,
intoxicated through the melting haze
of an icy, guava liquor.

Should you, should you, I mean really,
should you continue that dance
as a hooligan flaneur—of sorts—
strapped in the golden finery of a
rip-rollicking, countryside king (—fox—),
running, tripping, running, tripping
amidst a field so hazy it seems to
butter your bread with poppyseeds.

Will you, will you, I mean really,
you will finish the dance (eventually),
only to revive it with castanets—
enflamed, spiced, cherried and decorated,
adorned only
with fire, the fieriest of fingers.
These tickle arduous morning breath
as you look, glance, see that river cat
and
(I mean, really)
you truly, truly see it and dance.
(Again!)— ◆

James Dobbyn

AVO
CADO
GIRL

The day finally came when I had to sell my bathroom mirror. I was going to go cold-turkey, break my addiction once and for all. In retrospect, I could see how it had slowly taken over my life. I hardly went out anymore, except to buy food. I almost never washed. My hair was long and greasy. My nails were grimy and untrimmed. I had gone days and days without seeing another human face.

I became addicted one morning as I was brushing my teeth. Or, to be more exact, just after I had finished brushing them. I was getting ready for work, in the middle of my usual morning routine. I spat, rinsed, and pulled my lips back to examine my teeth. They looked normal, not an otherworldly toothpaste-commercial sparkling white but not particularly yellow, either. I opened my mouth wide to examine my molars, and as I did, something about the flesh inside my mouth caught my eye.

The delicate skin inside my right cheek looked particularly pink and juicy. In fact, my entire mouth was more striking and vibrant than I had remembered it. I leaned in and looked into the alien world, following the little spider-webbed veins inside my cheeks. Their tiny purple networks stretched across the walls of my mouth like riverbeds, branches, highway systems. They were more beautiful to me than any part of my face or body, or any face or body

I had ever seen. They were built from the food I ingested and carried my blood. Their pattern was encoded in my DNA. It was *my* saliva that glistened on their surface, rich with my particular menagerie of mouth-bacteria.

And the teeth! Those stark protrusions of bone, erupting out of the soft pink gum tissue, obelisks so elegant and blank against the roiling damp carpet of life! My life! I had built these myself, but their construction was like Stonehenge to me. They had dutifully ground up every piece of food I'd eaten since childhood, tearing apart hundreds of pounds of chicken and cow flesh, shearing through fields of broccoli and lettuce, and stoically enduring jawbreakers and ice cubes.

I didn't even call in sick to work. I stood in front of the mirror for eight hours that first day before hunger drove me away. From that point on, I hardly did anything else. I'd wake up in the morning and race to the bathroom, brush my teeth with irritated impatience, and open wide. Three days later, I was informed that I no longer had a job. I didn't bother picking my stuff up from the office.

I felt at home in my mouth. Looking at anything else bored and irritated me. I explored every nook and cranny with a single-minded fascination—for a while, the tongue, thick and meaty, was my object of fixation. It was so independent! I'd count each bud on its mottled surface, and when I was halfway through it would jump in a sudden flick! and I'd giggle and lose count. As weeks went by, I realised that each of my teeth had a different personality. Some, like my top-right second molar, were naturally shy. It didn't butt in and kept mainly to itself. Others took over the conversation, leaning into their neighbours insistently. Naturally, this caused some friction. But as engrossing as my teeth were, they could not approach the great mystery past the uvula. There, around that dark corner, lay the true secrets. More than anything, I yearned to go spelunking in that damp cavern, rappelling deep into the fragrant black. I spent many hours with a flashlight, trying to peer into the pink tunnel in myself. The angles never quite worked, even when I used a smaller hand-mirror. I could see the far wall of my throat, but the inner wall was beyond my reach. I longed to see the entrance to my lung system, just once.

For a while, I lived off my savings. The nagging thought of money haunted my 'free' time. At night, I thought only of the bills I hadn't paid, the chores I needed to do, and the friendly-concerned messages I hadn't responded to. I'd lie there, staring into the black, thinking that, yes, tomorrow would be the day, the day when I went out to look for a job, or at least for a walk. The more I thought these thoughts and the more I disappointed myself by abolishing my midnight resolutions the next day, the harder it became to do anything else. I felt the weight of the days building up on top of me, the weight of their sameness pushing me down.

When I did honour my resolutions, the result was nothing but more agony and disappointment. On these rare days, I began resisting the urge from the very moment I woke up and continued resisting it through every moment of the day. When I left my apartment and went out into the world, I was hopelessly lost. The people I passed on the street walked with a purpose, some destination in mind. They walked in groups, with friends, holding their lovers' hands or their dogs' leashes. I felt their eyes on me and fixed mine on the pavement ahead. Somehow, they knew I wasn't one of them. When I got back home, drained, with nothing to do and nowhere to go, I couldn't help but return to the mirror. In it, my face always looked fatter and older and sadder than before. All that was good about me was inside my mouth.

As my money began to run out, I sold the things I had accumulated in my apartment. The flatscreen TV was the first to go, being both expensive and useless. The tasteful oil paintings I'd so carefully selected and hung soon followed. Finally, all that was left was the futon and a blanket on the floor. And the mirror. I ate out of cans which I bought in bulk late at night once a month. My jaw ached all the time. I slept with my mouth open, and every morning I'd wake up parched.

So the day finally came when I had to sell it. There was no particular 'rock bottom'. I simply woke up one morning (it was 5PM) and, instead of turning towards the bathroom, sat down in the middle of my bare apartment. Nothing moved. No time passed through me. I sat, thinking about how it would feel to smash the mirror—would I be free?

No. I wouldn't smash the mirror. I would sell it. I found my phone under the futon. The battery was dead. It hadn't been turned on in days, maybe weeks. I dug the charging cable out of a drawer and plugged it in. After a minute, it lit with a buzz. I still had the app I used to sell the furniture, now all I needed was a picture of the mirror. I took it from off to the side without looking into it. Then I began a title for the post. 'BATHROOM MIRROR,' it said. 'Excellent condition. Must pick up.' I stopped. I hadn't thought of what to ask for in exchange. I couldn't remember how much it had cost in the first place. I could ask for anything, as long as it was worth less than a bathroom mirror.

I knew what I wanted.

I hadn't seen an avocado in two years, but my eyes still

remembered that rough, veiny, dark-dark-green skin, the colour of thick moss. I felt my thumb push into the just-ripe-enough flesh of its flank, and the little bit of give in its firmness. I saw my knife sliding around its ovoid equator, a bit of thin green residue clinging to the blade. I felt the two halves separate with a little twist, and saw the perfect clean pit-shaped depression in the yellow-green of one half. Then, in one stroke, the glinting knife biting down into the pit, and with one twist setting it free. Yes, it had to be an avocado.

It was unnerving how quickly I received a reply to my ad. As if someone was out there already, waiting with an avocado, in need of a mirror. My other half. They simply said, 'I would like to trade my avocado for your mirror. I can come to you. What is your address?' I sent the stranger my information. The reply came: 'I will be along shortly.'

I took the mirror down from the bathroom wall without looking into it and leaned it facedown against the wall by the door. I went into the bedroom and picked some cleaner clothes, or at least less-recently-worn clothes, out of a trash bag. I found the stump of an old deodorant stick and smeared it under my arms. It clung whitely to the hairs. I felt the impulse to check my hair, and looked into the bathroom. The blank wall gave me an alien feeling of satisfaction. I forced a small dab of toothpaste from its squeezed-out husk of a tube and brushed. I hadn't brushed yet today, and I felt relief in doing it now. The buzzer sounded. I hurried to the door and buzzed the stranger in. A minute later, there was a knock at my door.

It was a girl. She was shorter than me and somewhat younger, with black hair. She wore faded jeans and a pair of beat-up canvas flats. She stared at me for a long time, both hands plunged in the pocket of a shapeless sweatshirt. I didn't move. Her dark eyes scanned the bare, dim room behind me. Her face was blank, impassive, yet in the silence she seemed to radiate that strange satisfaction I felt looking at the wall where the mirror used to be. We stood there for a long time. Then, she pulled one small pale hand from the pocket of her sweatshirt and extended it to me. In it was an avocado.

She took the mirror and left without a word. All that remained of her was a faint tinge in the air of a sweet, musky perfume which I cannot name or describe. It reminded me of something far, far back in my childhood, a bright room and a woman. I wanted to call her back, but she was gone. Soon, the scent was, too. I was alone in the room with the avocado. It was just like the one I had pictured: clean, rough, and the deepest green, without any mouldy white patches on the end. I squished my thumb into its side, and it yielded just enough. I closed my eyes, turning it over in my hands. I pictured the pit inside, snug in its bed of fruit. From in there, everything must sound muffled. All dark. Even the jostling from truck to ship to crate would be dull and softened. I squeezed it again. No soft spots, no hollow pits of rot. Good. There would be no black or grey inside, only that delicious shade of light green, with a few blotches of yellow near the centre. I set it down on the counter next to the sink.

In a drawer I found a large knife—the handle was coming apart. I flicked on the overhead light and washed the knife in the sink, rubbing the blade with my fingers and picking off bits of grime with my nails. I shut off the water and shook it dry, flinging droplets into the sink. The knife gleamed as I turned it over. I saw my face in the blade, blurred and stretched. I closed my eyes.

Without any more hesitation, I picked up the avocado and slid the blade into it lengthwise, along the side. I pivoted it around the pit, drawing it through the tough skin with ease. The pit felt hard and slick against the edge of my knife. I sliced around the fat end first, working my way to the skinny end until there was a single cut running all the way around the avocado. I set the knife down on the counter. Holding the bottom half with my left hand, I twisted the top with my right and pulled it away.

Inside the avocado, where the pit should have been, there was a mirror. Or rather, it was as if the pit had been coated in a chrome mirror-finish, polished to a bright sheen. It bulged out of the green flesh like an eyeball, clean and silver. In it, I saw my face, stretched over the orb-like surface, my eyes flared. Adrenaline shot through me and I dropped the two halves with a scream. Stumbling back, I tripped over a trash bag and fell hard onto the floor. I curled up, wrapping my elbows over my face, hyperventilating.

When I was finally able to sit up, I saw that my legs were shaking. I was shivering all over. My back to the avocado, I looked around. Nothing was different. Everything was as it had been for months, apart from the blank piece of wall over the sink. Seeing that blank space again, I slowly stopped shivering. It was real. I felt exactly like that pure white rectangle.

I turned around to look at the avocado. The two halves lay right where I'd dropped them. From across the room, I could see the glint of the pit. It was real, too. I crawled toward it, brushing trash bags out of the way. When I was an arm's length away, I stopped and straightened up. They were like a hand and a glove, the one with its chrome protuberance and the other with its yellow-green crater. The hollow one was nearest me, and this I reached for first, gingerly touching its skin with the tips of my fingers. I brought it up to eye-level. On closer inspection, it was nothing but a normal half of an avocado. It was unusually pristine, but not so perfect as to appear fake. I ran my index finger along the surface of its flesh. It felt soft and slippery, and left a bit of residue on me. I sniffed it. It didn't smell like much of anything. Slowly, I dipped my finger into the hollow in its centre and stroked the floor of the depression.

I placed the half back on the floor, skin side down. It tilted to my right and came to rest. Then I turned my attention to the other half. Its spotless mirror-sheen was almost unbelievable, considering it had been encased in avocado just a few minutes before. Again, I saw my face stretched and distorted in its oval bulge. I kept my mouth closed. Just as carefully as before, I picked it up and touched its fruit with the tip of one finger. Nothing happened. I stared at it for a while. I realised I was staring into my own eyes, reflected in the pit. I wanted to examine its other half, the one buried under the green. Normally, I would extract an avocado pit with the blade of a knife, but this seemed impossible. An idea presented itself. Without hesitation, I leaned forward and sunk my teeth in, closing my mouth around the smooth, cold pit and biting it clean out. I rolled it around in my mouth, detaching chunks of avocado with my tongue. I tasted only the delicate flavour of avocado.

I swallowed. Before I had time to think, it was slipping down my oesophagus into my gut. I sat there for a minute, still kneeling, the chomped-out shell of the avocado in my hand. I could feel the pit, like a large pill, sliding down into my body. I wasn't thinking anything. After a minute, I got to my feet.

I opened the front door and went out into the hall, walked to the end of the hallway and smoothly descended the two flights of stairs. I pushed open the door at the bottom and stepped out onto the street. It was just getting to be dusk, and the air was cool and bluish. There was no one around. I turned right and walked barefoot down the pavement to a low wall adjacent to the building. Behind it, there was a courtyard with a tree whose leaves were just beginning to yellow.

I leaned back against the wall and listened to the wind in the tree. I am listening to the wind in the tree. ◆

YOUR FACE LOOKS GOOD ON ME, KATE TOWSEY

◂ IN FAKE EDEN, AUDREY LEE

ANA-
(IN LAST RESORT)

Sebastian McKimm

'Haptic,' from the Greek *aptô* (to touch), does not designate an extrinsic relation of the eye to the sense of touch, but a 'possibility of seeing [*regard*],' a type of vision distinct from the optical [...] As Maldiney says; 'in the spatial zone of closeness, the sense of sight behaves just like the sense of touch, experiencing the presence of the form and the ground *at the same place*'.

—Deleuze, *The Logic of Sensation*

...before my eyes many times
She has seen her—gripping frozen
wilt into *Collapse*

Before, I saw her. You don't understand! *I saw her in Theresienstraße*
Lying limp, frail liver-spotted fist clenched in my hand, for I couldn't
let it fall

Open—Again,
Under a ceramic scrape
someone is choking.
Angled clutter, *Scrape*
Knife falls—*collapses*.
Spreads and drips, in dribbles

Then thin streams, off the table's edges…

Held her in my regard so cold to the warm touch, frozen
We pulled her closer, to centre wave reverberations, like a sigh
By my
To touch. to stop-up But could not, already no passage, no
access—*heave-hold-heave*
Convulsing… *by your side.*

Heterochromia names it an anomaly, and so my mother's green and
blue eye, blue-green eyes turn her world cold in stark horror. The
way each white transitions in hues—one, moss-like, crowds a verdant
thicket; bowled aquamarine basin to turquoise shallows, rings lightly
their darkness vanishing, taking inward, grazing blackness closer like
the call of precipice
vanishing distances into seconds into *ligh-*
St-op! *Do something...*
Echoes unexpected in canon, watched not alone in multiplicity—cyanic
Please do something!

Poised in elegance if freeze-framed, a diver in centripetal acceleration
We spin inward into moments, compressing into a dancer stretching
Downward, limply inward to the earth at her toes—clenched-in into folded
overlap, we latch her to herself, shell-like, clutching for safety in water
And Please *heave—breath*e
'Extend *and up*: Reach for the skies…'

Splash.

So she sinks and is forced to ease out
with gravity—compression tilted to extract
A splatter suffices but

Both times good fortune was made

palpable. Chest compression restoration
of this machine, duly reanimated

She broke three ribs that day. *That's what* I *wanted to* avoid, says *Theresienstraße… I saw her lying* gripped by *Angles*
She told me of the white of winter, how street and screaming sky, vanishing, become one. Became Angel. *Crack.*
Breathing—Reanimated by screaming. Atme!

...Crack.

WER, wenn ich schriee, hörte mich denn...
Menschen nicht *...Crack.*
Try shriek with no passage. Remorselessly held close, *in* regard, *a beat* resurfaces—skin-level in a *limp*-wrist, vertiginously losing hold of your *grip*
Fingers clutching

She left, limp, in my limp arms. You don't understand... I cannot. Again. *I cannot stand... I held her, absent. I cannot give to*—to see her like this—*cannot take it again...*

▪

On his forest walks, Herr V. and his machine would whisper sweet childhood melodies,
Tunelessly meandering dry lips along the cyclical hymn from the music box—
The one with the little alpine boy and his dog, broken now, from winding
Animated in too eager repetition.

Toward the end, when he was very sick, he would get up by one slow
Step, and on that bench at the shrine by those pines there—get up, dutifully, to pray. His Whispers pressed close to the weather-worn crucifix

For truly he believed that otherwise, he once told me, his *Herrgott* would struggle to hear him. Grazing with his prayers, salvation beckoning away—*fromm*!

▪

Cricothyrotomy, she calls it coolly. *It is your duty to intervene*
Four minutes without oxygen, her breathless tune one I will remember.

In last resort, pick soft flesh between sonorous apples, and valleys,
    and mostly skin
And even with pen-casings and tubes, scraping with knives, but not straws
In last resort: intubate.
Break open the pressure, ease back the lining. Black hole gazing
    inward, *Convulsing*.
Tunelessly lips relieve Machine whistle wheezing—Palpitation
Forced to interface to oxygen, re-opened by casing, to whisper,
to closer, to prayer, to *Breathe* to
Please—Again ◆

NARIYAL

Sona Popat

water carrier:
a sacred centre and
palms pressed together like
the sugar clinging to fingertips and rind.

water carrier:
upon your shoulder a wicker-basket full
of stories from then, the names of faces
that look a lot like ours.

water carrier:
three eyes drawn with a steady hand
in hand as you walk surely,
circling the fire.

water carrier:
energy and oxygen
cracked open and poured past
your lips straight through to—

water carrier:
connecting the clouds
to the earth
with skin stretched over life. ◆

OFFSHORE CHOREOGRAPHIES, MARIA KAMINSKA

2019: AN AMERICAN CHILDHOOD

Elle Lavoix

Her first bikini is white.

She didn't want to buy it at first. The elastic waistband dug into her skin, nudging a roll of fat over the top. And anyway, don't white swimsuits become see-through when you get wet? But her friends, eagerly crowded in the changing room with her as a Katy Perry song vibrated through the shop, insisted white looked *so good* on her skin.

West Palm beach is crowded, dotted with bright red, yellow and blue parasols sprouting towards the sun. Children are frenziedly splashing in the water, emitting high pitched shrieks, infected by the giddiness of early summer. Up on the beach, middle-aged parents are eagerly undressing, revealing their parched, pasty winter skin to the sun.

Over her shoulder, her mother sits erect on a folding chair, her bony knees pressed together, sunscreen coating her porcelain cheeks, a wide-brimmed straw hat stiffly guarding her head. Clutched between her fingers is the Palm Beach Post, a mugshot of a haggard Jeffrey Epstein leering out from the front page. Every few minutes, she peers over the top of the paper, as if to ensure Kelly is still there, still within reach, still unharmed.

And Kelly is still there, lying on a fluffy pink beach towel, scanning the scene around her, waiting for the right moment to take her clothes off. Originally she had packed the Coors Light towel her friend's dad had given her during a barbecue, but her mom had found the item in her bag before leaving the house and promptly thrown it out.

She decides to undress lying down. This, she hopes, will both minimize the number of people that can watch the unveiling process, while ensuring her stomach looks flat to those that can. But the process is less slick than she imagined. Her shorts stubbornly hug her hips, dragging the bikini bottom down and revealing timid beginnings of pubic hair. Mortified, she yanks up the waistband and tugs the back of her shorts down.

Shorts and T-shirt removed, she feels the warmth of the sun caress her stomach. She realizes she has never exposed her stomach to the sun, except perhaps in one rare moment as a toddler, when she broke free from her mother and ran around naked. And here she is, revealing her brown stomach to the whole wide world, letting it bulge over the taut, white bikini bottom. The bikini bottom that will become see through when she goes in the water. Revealing the pubic hair.

She balls up her T-shirt and shorts and places them under her head, letting her long curls bounce down on either side of her towel. She slides on her new sunglasses, the ones with the leopard-skin frames that she bought with the bikini. *So hot,* her friends said.

Kelly recalls the awkward discussion she had had with her mother about Jeffrey Epstein. Her mother had called her into the kitchen after school one day. Staring intently at the chamomile tea she was cradling between her hands, her knee bouncing up and down under the table, her mother had asked her whether girls did things like that in her school. 'Things like that' meant going off with rich old men. Ever since Kelly had hit puberty, she had sensed her mother's fear growing stronger. It made her think of a child finding themselves eye-to-eye with a Rottweiler.

But Kelly didn't really know the girls that did that. They were the popular girls, the blonde ones who got their periods early and got Snaps from the cute guys at school. She didn't tell her mom about those girls. But massaging older men for money was just so gross.

Through her sunglasses she sees a boy saunter up to a navy blue towel spread a few feet away. His skin is shimmering bronze despite it only being early July, and fat drops of seawater run in rivulets down his chest. He looks slightly older than her, maybe fifteen or so, with tousled brown hair, dimples and a faint dusting of fuzz on his upper lip. She presses her thighs together and inches to the right to see him better. He puts on his headphones and lies down facing her, his eyes engrossed in his phone. A sun-bleached lock of hair falls over his forehead and he shakes his head, water from his locks spraying in the air.

She tries to remain cool, prays her mother has not noticed her reaction to the newcomer.

But the newcomer seems to have little interest in anything besides his phone. She sees a smile spread across his face as he grips the phone more tightly. The smile strikes her as self-satisfied. Like he is giving deep, silent approval to whatever he is watching.

Kelly puts on her headphones and swipes through her iPhone until she settles on a song. Her mom hates the song, and especially the music video that goes with it. The one where the rapper and his friends shoot whipped cream onto the bent-over asses of women in thong bikinis. But the women's asses are blurred out, and even though it's all kind of weird, Kelly doesn't really see what the big deal is.

Then again, her mom is pretty uptight about most things. Kelly figures it has to do with her dad. She has never known him, knows only that he abandoned her mom for another woman before she was born. That, she understood from her mom, was what black men did.

'Kelly?' she hears her mom say. She is straightening out her sundress and pressing the straw hat down onto her head. 'I'm going to the bathroom, okay? You just stay here.'

Her mom's movement distracts the newcomer, whose eyes detach from the screen and meet hers. She blushes and looks away.

But the newcomer doesn't. He keeps looking at her, his gaze piercing into her body. She feels her muscles slacken under the gaze, the nervous contractions in her buttocks disappearing. When she finally gathers up the courage to look back at him, he breaks out into a wide grin, displaying teeth so white they look translucent.

Her heart leaps into her throat and she musters a shy smile back. He gestures to her, beckoning to her and patting his towel. She freezes, then feels her body tremble like a petrified puppy. She can only imagine what her mother would say if she came back to find her sitting on an older boy's towel. The boy shrugs, his hazel eyes laughing at her, then turns back to his phone.

Her mother returns relaxed, telling Kelly to go get some ice cream. Kelly weighs the pros and cons of the offer. She loves ice cream, especially gooey vanilla ice cream in a wafer cone, loves the way it melts over the edge of the cone and makes her fingers sticky. But getting up would mean baring her body not only to the whole beach, but to the boy. And eating ice cream meant cheating on her diet. She'd have to own up to it in her diet app, and then she'd have to punish herself with a lemon juice fast the day after.

She decides to settle for a Diet Coke, then pulls the tropical sarong out of her beach bag and uses her chin to hold it against her chest as she knots it on the back. She sees the boy look up, and as she hurries away to the drinks stand, feels his gaze follow her.

The drink seller banters about the weather, the first real day of summer, how white everyone on the beach is. She doesn't bother to point out his racial obliviousness. As she turns around, she finds herself face to face with the boy.

'Hi,' he says, his mouth breaking into a grin, his eyes laughing at her. 'I'm Sebastian.'

Her breath catches as she clutches her Diet Coke, drops of cool condensation sliding between her fingers.

'Hi,' she says nervously, looking at the ground. The lid of the Coke pops off the drink.

'What's your name?' he continues, smiling.

'Kelly,' she whispers, trying to replace the lid.

'Hey Kelly, relax. I'm a cool guy. Even my mom says so,' he jokes.

She cracks a smile and lifts her eyes.

'You here with someone?'

'Yeah, my mom.'

'Oh man, that sucks. My dad lets me come here on my own.'

Kelly feels her shoulders relax a little. 'My mom'd never

let me do that! She never lets me out of her sight.'

'Well, you're kinda out of her sight now,' he says, looking around slyly. 'You go to school here?'

'Yeah. I'm going to high school next year. What about you?'

'Oh, I go to high school in California. I'm just here visiting my old man for the summer. He has a house over here.'

That's why I haven't seen you around town, she thinks. 'Nice,' she says.

'You wanna get outta here?'

'Outta here?' she says blankly. 'I can't. My mom's waiting for me.'

'Well, maybe not right now. Another day.' His eyes bore into hers. She feels naked despite the tightly knotted sarong. 'Give me your number.'

▪

At home she puts Katy Perry's 'Bon Appétit' on as she showers, still wearing the bikini. When she steps out of the bikini bottom, it snaps at her wrist.

Got me spread like a buffet

Bon a, bon appétit, baby

She hums as she rinses the bikini bottom, squeezing it, turning it inside out. She notices the white streaks on the inside panel of the bottom, and hastily scrubs them off.

Melt in your mouth kind of lovin'

Bon a, bon appétit, baby

When she steps out of the shower, the bathroom is filled with mist, the mirror clouded. She hits pause on the music and sees a notification from Sebastian pop up on her phone.

Hey there.

She wraps her hair up in a towel and unlocks the phone.

Are you back home yet? I wanted to show you something.

She is still wet, fat drops of water trickling down her front, between her breasts, over the curves of her stomach. She sees a link appear under his message.

Open the link, he urges.

She looks at the URL and hesitates. There is no thumbnail, but she clicks on it anyway.

The page opens and she sees three white men standing around a naked, heavily made up black woman on her knees. A long, synthetic black wig hangs down to her hips, tangled and knotty. The men are fully dressed, but their flies are open and they are gripping their cocks, eyes closed and heads thrown back, spraying white onto the wig and the woman's thick, curly eyelashes. A drop is slowly sliding off the tip of her nose.

She feels her throat go dry, then feels a rush of vomit. But even as bile fills her mouth, she is unable to stop looking at the woman's nose. The drop reminds her of vanilla ice cream, dribbling off the end of a cone.

She sees another notification from Sebastian arrive at the top of the screen, covering the closed eyes and open mouths of the men, and despite her growing angst, she clicks on it.

Did you like it? :-)

She stares weakly at the message, not wanting to believe this message came from him, the beautiful bronzed boy with the teeth so white they looked transparent. She sees him typing, then pausing, then typing again. She knows already she does not want to receive another message, but cannot bring herself to look away.

Then:

That's what I want us to do.

She stares blankly at the mirror in front of her. Hanging from the shower head behind her is the bikini, translucent, dangling, fat drops of water sliding down the straps.

She sends her response.

;-)

◆

BODY, REMEMBER

Lily Bayntun-Coward

Σώμα, θυμήσου όχι μόνο το πόσο αγαπήθηκες,
όχι μονάχα τα κρεββάτια όπου πλάγιασες,
αλλά κ
Body, remember not only how oft you were sexed
not only the beds upon which you were lain
but also*
how vast they yawned, suddenly, and stretched,
afterwards, with you clung atop his chest
while he slept.

Body and soul, know that to be gifted wholesale
did not leave you more valued.
So, too,
now that all this belongs to the past
remember, body
though as he reached for you through the dark
love came clear and unclaimed,
the two are not one and the same. ◆

* The first three lines and their translation are taken from 'Body, remember' by Constantine Cavafy.

DOWNSTAIRS LIVING ROOM, OLUWASEMILORE DELANO

GOOD MORNING SUNSHINE

Kathryn Ellis

The challenge, in one's thirties,
[34 next birthday. Still putting toothpaste on my spots]
is to consider a dead houseplant without turning it into a
[clunking]
metaphor.
It would
[I decide, as I sip my coffee and gaze in a mournful,
sleep-clogged sort of way at the desiccated spines of my
poor ficus]
be particularly unhelpful to imagine two of the rounder
leaves as
[a pair of withered]
emblems of my elderly ovaries.
[I am dressed in pyjamas at two o'clock on a bright Saturday]
Equally,
[I decide]
matters would unlikely improve if I were to construct a
[sustained]

narrative around my inability to keep even one small green cutting alive.

[and the imaginary ramifications of this particular incompetence should I ever, in fact, manage to reproduce]

But it comes like a wave,

[in clichés, then?]

this anxious storytelling: an eddying cacophony of worst-case scenarios and imaginative catastrophising.

[Would it really be that bad if I never managed to replicate my dubious genetic material in miniature? Wouldn't it be far worse, for example, to trip on the loose lip of the hall carpet, smash my jaw on the windowsill, and walk around with half a face for the rest of my life?]

I grope for the coffee jug

[or to forget every word I ever knew besides 'webinar' and 'knuckles', and be compelled to repeat them at a screeching pitch every time I came across a brown-eyed man?]

and splash in another muddy trickle,

[who thought it would be a good idea to give me a plant to look after, anyway? I once dropped a paving slab on a guinea pig by accident. I am not to be trusted with living things.]

and bring the mug to my lips.

Smile, says the mug.

And I do, because— ◆

CHINATOWN
牛车水游客询

UNCLES IN SINGAPORE, SOLAL BAUER

Imani Thompson

SISTERS LIKE US

There is a doll. There are three photographs. There is a pink hat. There is one unused lipstick and one that I bought her. Both are red. There is an iPod, but we have lost the charger. There are straighteners with stickers on them, two of the Jonas Brothers. There is a bitten pencil.

She liked the doll because it looked like her. Well, that's what people said. It has green trousers that you can take off and put back on—the velcro is worn from this. The top is purple, with a star on the front, and the doll's skin is brown. The twisted hair that never stays put, that's its best feature. She called it her, *Shantel* doll. I told her that this was narcissistic—but without using the word because I didn't know it.

Not that any of this is important. What is important is that it is September and birds are singing.

I say this because Hannah (a counsellor) told me to look out for things like this: seasons and birds. She seems to think that they are important. I wanted to tell her that her opinions are often trash, but she also says that I am confrontational and I would hate to prove her right.

What season is it where you are? What are the birds doing? Maybe you care.

I am only looking out of the window to distract myself from looking inside. Tamir is hanging around the street again in his new car: silver this time, no roof this time, loud music like all times. He is the most beautiful man that I have ever seen. You would agree if you saw him. He's like Adam in the garden just as God curled his final eyelash. His skin is so dark you might expect to look up from it and see the moon.

He slides from the car, arms bare. *Mmm, M'ama* look at him. He's going to see Kophie who lives across from us. She's skinny, pretty—if you're into that sort of thing.

This would be a much better day if he was coming to knock on my door; but I don't have any beautiful men for you. I wouldn't even have any food for you, or a drink, so you'd have wasted your visit. We couldn't go into the kitchen see, 'cause my dad's in there. Normally there'd be fried pie, biscuits, okra, ice-cream, corn bread, all the good stuff. But now there's just him with his clothes on from yesterday, making this noise like a dog being repeatedly kicked.

But I'm not looking inside.

Kophie has come to the door. She's wearing a leather skirt that only just holds her in; shiny hoops. I like her braids. Her boobs got so much bigger this summer that Shantel said she must have got them done. Shantel was always saying things like that. Once, Tamir had taken her for a drive, kissed her, and never texted her again. The following week he started seeing Kophie—who Shantel thought was her friend. So she hates Kophie, hated—doesn't matter.

▪

Tamir waits on the step, lights a blunt. Kophie comes back with what looks like lemonade.

Our mum came to the funeral (the lemonade reminded me). But to understand why that was significant I'd have to tell you other things, sad things; and I already have so much sadness that I keep thinking the floor will fall through for the weight of me. Maybe the ground is used to sadness. That's what Dyani says. She says that it sucks it all up, but that one day, when no-one's looking, it will spit it back out.

I'd rather talk to Dyani than Hannah; but the Church is paying for Hannah and my aunt says I have to go because when people are nice it's best to be nice back. I say when people are mean is it okay to be mean back, and she says no. But before she says no she gets this look in her eye like she wants to kill someone.

Eurgh, come off it. Kophie and Tamir are sucking on each other's faces like they're zombies in the apocalypse.

'Miriam, Miriam.' That's my dad calling me.

'Yeah?' I shout back.

'Miriam would you… I can't find her…'

I watch the kitchen door. He keeps shouting my name

then not wanting anything.

'Dad?'

No reply. The door doesn't move.

They're still getting off. Maybe if I stare at them long enough they'll stop. By the power of Professor X I'll—*shit*. Tamir's staring at me. He's standing and staring at me staring at him. He takes a step off the porch onto the grass. *Shit*. Kophie's saying something to him and making a face but he ignores her and keeps staring. *What should I—*

He starts to wave. Slowly, hesitantly. Then he tries a smile but stops, moves his palm over his chest, over his heart. He looks like he's trying to speak.

He's so beautiful and what he's doing is so strange that I feel funny inside. Not the sort of funny you'd expect when the most beautiful man you've ever seen is paying you attention; but a sort of funny that makes me want the ground to spit back all its sadness. Right here. Right now. (Only I'm looking.)

I duck down under the windowsill. Count to ten. By the time I look back he's gone, as is Kophie; but the two glasses are there so it must have been real.

The night that Shantel went for the drive with Tamir she wore this yellow dress and looked so pretty. The sort of pretty you look when you like someone and you think they like you, and it's like anything in the whole world can be yours.

I lie now with my stomach flat on the couch, my face in a pillow. That's enough of outside. That's enough of inside. That's enough of everything.

I don't know why I'm talking to you like you care. I know you've only found me by accident. My aunt said that everyone cared about Michael Brown when he got shot in Missouri. There were media reports, then reports on those media reports. It was all over Facebook. People were angry at the cop that shot him, people cried.

'We're only one state over from Missouri,' said my aunt, with that look in her eye. Well, actually Shantel had been on the state border when it happened. She'd been on the state border, speeding (they said).

I turn my face into the room. There is a blue notebook that we haven't opened. There are denim shorts. There is a textbook on Algebra. There are hair clips still in their plastic.

I don't know why my dad keeps taking things out of her room and putting them on the carpet. I think I will ask him to stop. The doll is in the middle of it all. Keeps staring at me.

Reminds me of this day, a hot day, when Shantel and I had gone into a shop, both of us sucking on ice pops. She ran over to this stand, so excited because there were other dolls of the same brand. All these dolls with hair that didn't stay put. She stared at them for a long time with her eyes all squinty, then left the shop and said that it was silly because she couldn't look like *all* of them. At the time, the only thing I thought was important was my ice pop; but now I think other things. I think about how, if she'd looked like a different doll, on hot days I'd still have someone to suck ice pops with. I'll just never stop thinking about this.

Dyani says that if a spirit is angry they may stay around and haunt the place. Shantel had a big temper so yesterday I went to her favourite shop at the mall, but she wasn't there. Today I'll go and see if she's at the park. I'll sit on the swings 'til dark if I have to. ◆

WEST VIRGINIA, 2019, JOE WILLS

WEST VIRGINIA, 2019, JOE WILLS

FORGIVE ME, SACRED EMILY & GERTRUDE (DOUBLE-SONNET ON AVOIDING POETS' GIVEN NAMES)

Cecily Fasham

'How do you do I forgive you everything and there is nothing to forgive.'
– Gertrude Stein, *Sacred Emily*

How now red cow No.
Do to you the things I
You to do the I things
Do things I the you to
I don't know if I'd
Forgive me any day I'd
You but this no thing done
Everything & every day
& no day I'm in love &
There are two of you who
Isn't a rose is a rose isn't every

Nothing stuck beneath a leg
To wish to wish & to forget
Forgive I meant to not to do.

Forgive forget forget-me-not the colour blue enfolding
To surround you in a sudden flood of pigment, there is
Nothing in this place that you cannot undo & yet & yet
Is somewhere you could so unsew unsex & so & sew & slow
There is a pause to take to undertake to reading you
& you, my pair of lovers in between your loosened limbs is
Everything but I don't want to pry to watch or to undress
You like some false voyeur who cares about your sex life O
Forgive me for the words I use I know that they are vulgar but
I get protective of you women I could never know, I wonder
Do you ever think of me some future self who re-assembles
You out of your humanhood into some languaged being

Do you know the way I'm meant to use your words to do it
How then if you know & if you (no) & now I'd ask I'd
ask you—how? ◆

ANNA AKHMATOVA, NOW AVAILABLE IN TECHNICOLOUR

Cecily Fasham

You come,
Clothed in your bright paint your grey Soviet garb,
Wearing your grief, your fear, your avant-garde
In bold unabstract pride—constructivist or not, I love
You in your sudden slam; you colour in the old land
I had dreamed in blocks of sepia-tones & drab:
You've dipped your feet in bowls of red & yellow paint
before you
Come & daub the cobbles in now, dance them back to life
With all your brilliantine words turning the East to blue,
To white,
Before the snow falls & obscures. ◆

UNTITLED #2, GROZ

POSTPARTUM

Tilly Alexander

must you why must you be
such unruly children   recoiling
from bathwater that is
so fragrant so
lovingly scented with lavender
or from
your occasional outfits the
stiff navy trousers or
yellow floral dress and
teeny tiny mary
janes that
I've always dreamed
of putting you in   until I finally do
& you become
these awful
awful
indescribable little brats

pouting at your straitjackets
refusing
to do anything but fall
entirely silent, else burst out
with far too large
          & inappropriate an emotion
for the moment, making me feel
          the most terrible parent
in the world for putting you &
myself worst of all
through this ordeal
again & again when
          will I learn
and why does no one tell you
          or maybe they do
          they definitely do actually
and you just don't listen   you think
          well I'll be good at it
but why does no one try harder
to stop you   why &
          who on earth decided this
was worth it, all these births
these upturned nights
like exorcisms
the worry that constantly

nibbles at you
& it makes it worse of course
to compare yours to other people's
            invariably
always doing better
look at them so beautiful so well-behaved
            I bet they fall asleep right away
I bet they never
puncture
that consecrated stillness
of night   not once
have they thrown their homemade food
peas & carrots specially
blended
to the ground, Eliot's children
are so smart   everyone whispers
and so impeccably dressed
look
            at their little velvet pinafores
            and how sweetly
            they play with the cat,
& O'Hara's, Oh
O'Hara's sing
so beautifully they are bursting
with emotion

in all the right ways
&
Dickinson's
they're strange and
a bit jittery, sure
but aren't they pretty
in their tightly coiled plaits!
don't they just
have the biggest eyes
the deepest souls
you've ever seen?
& meanwhile mine
mine
are met on the playground with
quite different whispers
from the other mothers & fathers
look at hers
how shabbily dressed
they are today
couldn't she at least
have got a comb through their hair?
          what do you expect though they're
caesarean babies   wrenched out
unwilling
poor things

they have bad bones—
these things
I know because
they tell me
these children
            in the way that children do
not meaning to be hurtful
& despite it all their
shortcomings
            I feel I must protect them
screen them
from these outside eyes   these
harsh opinions
            mine included
all the time worrying
that all these silent evaluations
infiltrate you
my darlings
are probably what
            will fuck you up the most
in the end
I should be grateful
after all the false starts
            to have children with
ten fingers & ten toes

these children mine who seem not
            to possess one iota
of talent
between them & yet whom
I love
shall always
love fiercely despite
it all, & could not ever give up hoping for ◆

A SOLDIER, KILLED AT SUNRISE

Ben Webb

The sun was so bright
at eight this morning—
it pierced the crack of dawn
and hit me, and halved my face.
One side like Moses to look at,
the other a dark absence, in exile. ◆

SHE WONDERS HOW UNCOMMON

Hannah Rice

It is not uncommon to assume that night is dark and sky is black and the colours of the world are nocturnal too but here it is orange from the streetlight beside her window and trees are navy leather and the moon is bright and uninterrupted and the night still smells of the day's August heat and it will not stop touching her in her head now it is July three weeks into the summer holiday it is evening and she is drunk from wine lying on the grass with a boy who is tall who is going to be influential one day who wears shirts with buttons without occasion

she wonders how uncommon it is that there is not the time to say I haven't done this before not with a boy just with fingers and thumbs instead there is just speed his fluid hands fluent hands she closes her eyes she tries to touch him where she should her hands are not fluent not fluid she wonders how uncommon it is to want it to be over she wonders how uncommon it is to want to be dead whilst it's happening she hears the noises he makes and listens for the birds in the trees and the trains on the tracks a mile away that you can hear if it's quiet enough

she wonders how uncommon it is to still have your shoes on the first time she thinks about what would happen if a man with a dog a woman out jogging some ramblers lost on the fen saw her with this body on top of her so she counts to ten and it is still not over then he makes a noise and it is still not over she wonders how uncommon it is not to speak not to say a word nor want to nor believe anything would come out if she opened her mouth he cries like an animal in a trap and she believes it is over but his weight has not shifted she opens her eyes and the ripple of his hair frames the purpling sky as he lies his head on her shoulder perhaps four seconds passing so

before he pushes himself away stands up turns his back on her arranges his clothes and she watches his shoulders as he tucks zips slips fastens she wonders how uncommon it is to want to cry she does not move she knows she is half-undressed in the grass she stares at the painted clouds in the sky are you getting up she cannot think of the words it is not a yes/no question are you okay yes I need to leave yes me too she sits up and feels his eyes meet her wince he turns away as she dresses I'm going to go then he says he leans down he presses his mouth into her head as she shuffles her dress over her legs she nods as he leaves he says thank you she nods she does not stand up until she hears the car she feels uneasy on her feet she feels sick after too much sugar at a sleepover her clothes are back on they don't feel right on her body anymore she is two and a half miles from home along the fen road she picks up the wine

it is orange morning again at the end of summer the

room the bed the house is too hot and she wishes her fingers could touch nothing at all ◆

THE WALK OF LIFE, PEDRO VALÉRIO VIEIRA

CLEARANCE (SKYE, 2019)

E. L. Hallesy

Like something spilt
from a height,
shape conceals
the slowness of lichen,
quashed run-rigs
time has stroked flat
barely streak
the next hill over,

evening's hesitant
sun salt-bakes
the abandoned croft
in gritty sodden wind,
driving rain over
fudgy moss
to silver-grey sea

and the distant white
of the big house further up.

I walked six hours
to this dismantled place
and now I'm here
the sea is still
shouldered the same
side, tick-circled
grass weaves a mattress
in the blown-out hearth.

There! The hidden
purple of the marsh
orchid, petals ruched
like struck velvet;
I take a photo.
Light falls thickly,
blunting the scrub
with its sticky glaze.
The marsh orchid
doesn't want to live,
it cannot choose.
How can it be

all that you were

they tore you from,
roof to ash,
stone to seam,
making of a woman
an open mouth,
her wail her song,

and it still be here?
The wind grooming
the mouldered green
of the cliff edge
until it reaches
the empty croft, a pit
of outpoured scree,
an aperture. ◆

SHROUD, AUDREY LEE ▸

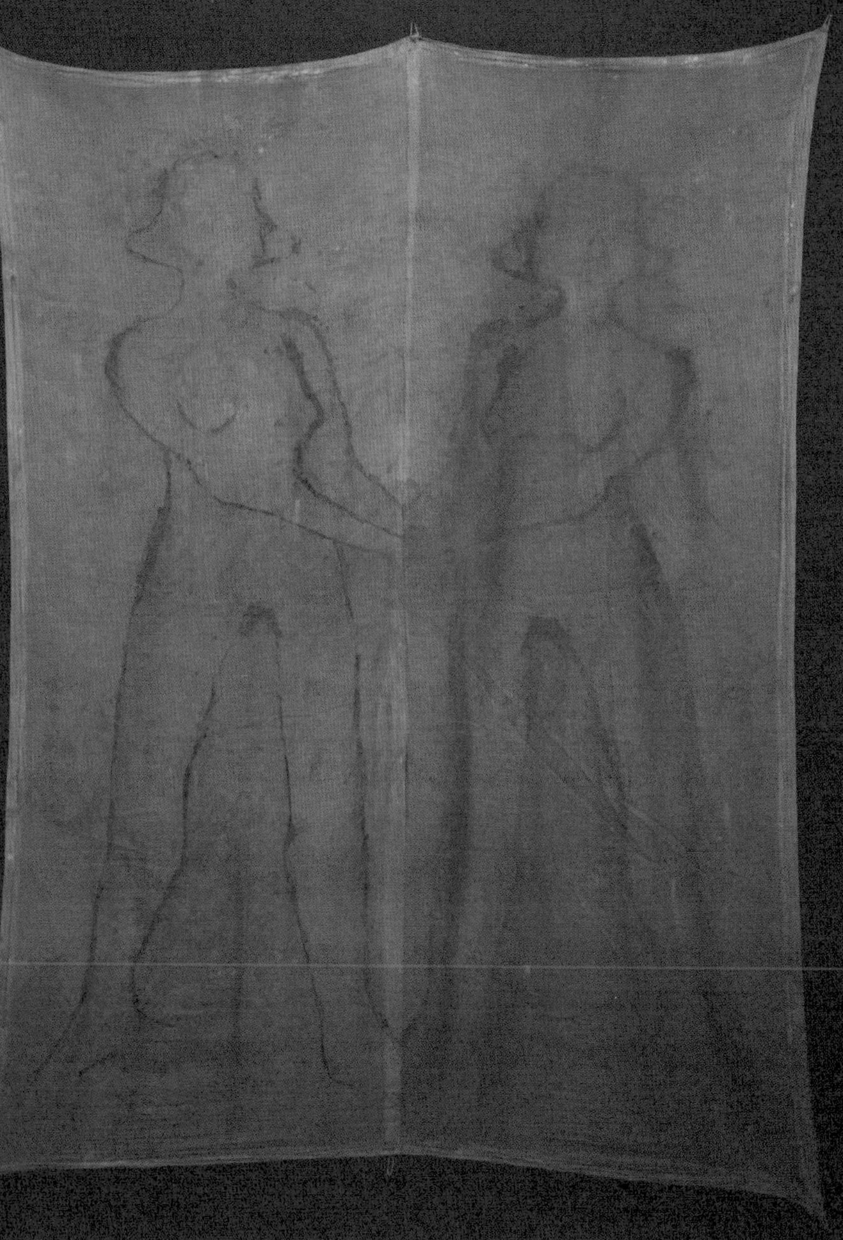

OYSTER CATCHER, 2019, DAVID SWARBRICK

MORE OR LESS

Paul Norris

October leaves
branches from your eye
and trains association to
a light on my notebook

to mark each day out of ten
words spread wide like wild
oats or margarine
across the suburbs

facing the city (palm to palm)
from time to time
I will tell you words
are nothing (like a game)

but life functions to resist
integration with the whole
that is something like a lie
I am in the middle of ◆

ELAINE

Georgie Newson-Errey

EXTRACT FROM *MARTENS' ENCYCLOPAEDIA OF SCIENCE*, JANUARY 2020

Robert Chester Wilson Ettinger (December 4, 1918 – July 23, 2011) was an American academic and physicist, known as 'the father of cryonics'. Ettinger founded the Cryonics Institute and the related Immortalist Society, and, until 2003, served as the groups' president. His body has been cryopreserved, along with the bodies of his first and second wives.

ARIZONA, USA, 24/06/3578

Eleven suns before seedingday, the excavation finally yielded. The sunsplit rock threw open its red mouthpit and all the little drillmen squirmed into the gapping like larvae. They'd been waiting on it for years now, glitching in the undergands as bitcode blazed overhead, and now it was finally here, the great symposium! The commonweb was all electrical with excitement, and who could blame them? Here were revivable relics from the Before Time, flesh and blood antecedents of everyself living and dead. What seemings would they be like? What news would they bring? What languages and storytells would be hidden in the roots of their teeth or jellies of their guts? It was impossible to tell, thought the commonweb. As the web dealt almost entirely in flickerings and possibilities, its ambivalence on the matter was, in no uncertain terms, a Big Fucking Deal. Back at the extraction site, the drillmen were sluicing the wound in a thick blue fluid that glittered and glossed like snakeskin, unlacing and retracing the threading black skywires. As the heat of the desert would have crisped up an unsuited body like a smashing of glass, there were few bystanders. Hours and days passed with only the wiring and sluicing and shivering heat, but in time the relics surfaced themselves and were carefully brought into the underglands. After the extraction came the revivaling. This was a painmaking process that spanned out over many loops of the clock, but a single sun before seedingday they found it: a heartbeat. The relic had been brought back from the great Plains of Timelessness, heaved up from the sick stomach of Apocalypse. It was giddying! It was unbrainable! The heat beat down on the flatplain and the wires sang up to the sun and when the masked clinician leading the revival asked the relic what its name was and it replied, in its taut small freeze-voice, 'Elaine,' the common-web lit up with a million fractallized signstrings, all whispering: Elaine! Elaine! Elaine!

THE FIRST BALLAD OF ELAINE

O Elaine, tell us now
Of the why and the how
Of your glittering nitrogen sleep!

First the fear it seared through
To the celluloid blue
And I fell to the swell of the deep.

O Elaine, were the glaciers whiter than white
And the icicles glycerol-sweet?

The frost glinted thick
On the dead and the quick
And the world it unfurled in retreat.

O Elaine, you must know
From your sleep in the snow
Of the white of the light of the mind.
You must know of the glow
That emits from below
When the nothing leaves nothing behind!

The light of the mind is gunmetal grey,
Watch it glint on the splinters of bone.
For there's nothing to do

In the expanse of You
But to cleave to the grief in the gloam.

O, there's nothing to see
In the expanse of Me
But the ache of surviving alone.

ARIZONA, USA, 29/06/3578

When Elaine looks up from her hands for the first time in two hours, the clinician is silhouetted against the doorway's frosted panel. She is talking to a silhouette that Elaine does not recognise, but their voices do not carry. Elaine watches the door for a few moments, wondering if the clinician is going to come in, but soon loses interest and stares down at her hands again. Various yellow wires have been inserted into her knuckles, which seem very pale in the white light. The wires are all gently pulsing, although not, Elaine notices, in time with her heartbeat. Elaine does not remember the wires being inserted, so it must have happened when she was sedated. Elaine does not know how many times she has been sedated.

The hands remind her of something that she cannot name or place, something from long ago. *Remember, Elaine.* She imagines her mind stretching over the endless absence like a bubble blown with gum, pulled so taut that it is almost translucent, reaching further and further until—pop!—the memory is located: a large, halved cantaloupe speared with cocktail sticks, which are themselves spearing a selection of yellow cubes. A cheese and pineapple hedgehog! People made them for children's birthday parties; they were the kind of thing that her mother would have deemed 'garish'. Elaine looks back at her hands, suddenly unable to connect the two images, and realises that she is crying, or something that feels like crying. The whole thing is just so absurd and stupid and beautiful: a cheese and pineapple hedgehog. Do they have pineapple here? Cheese? Hedgehogs? Elaine doesn't even know if they have outside anymore. Maybe this is all earth is now: white light and yellow wires.

The clinician's silhouette shifts and the door is pushed open. Hello, Elaine, she says, with a tight, bright smile. Elaine opens her mouth very slightly. We thought we should tell you, says the clinician, that a second resuscitation has been successful.

Elaine feels every muscle in her body tense. Her mind fills with a thick, deafening static, like a million guns going off at once; the static is not blue-grey, as it has been for all this frozen timelessness, but red, red, red. Robert, she says. The word sounds rough and desperate, as if she has clawed it into the air. The clinician looks at her with a poised, neutral expression that reveals neither pity nor contempt. A female, she says.

Every piece of hope inside Elaine falls away, dissonantly, like pennies on the ledge of a cascade game.

TWO SURGEONS

stand stiffly on the marbled staircase, their veils trembling in the breeze. I am simply unsure, the first surgeon is murmuring, if it was a judicious decision to revive them. There are already whisperings, you know.

There are always whisperings, says the second.

These are different, the first replies, his expression grim.

And why, sighs the second, would that be.

The first adjusts his collar. Clusters of the commonweb, he says, are suggesting that the relics were the kindred of Billionheirs.

The second furrows his brow and blows a jet of air through the gap in his front teeth. It makes a low whistling sound, and his veil flutters.

Ah, he says.

THE BILLIONHEIRS

Theologians, mythographers, philologists and other assorted Them of Letters generally concur that the Billionheirs were neither humanimal nor machine. Instead, they were composed entirely from a dizzying permutation of sugar and silicon, which is why they were all so smooth and white. They all lived separately together in a huge palace called Silicon Gorge, where the soil was creamclean and the sky was made of numbers. During the Great Collapse, when the seas spilled together to smelt the snow, the Billonheirs used their flying machines to escape to some other Elsewhere. This was strange, because these machines were the very same as those that had powered the un-powering that became the Collapse: huge sugarpillars that splintered into the sky until the horizon tightened around them like—well, even the drones had to admit that there was something erotic about it, didn't they? Three, two, one—we have lift off! The plasma-thick cloud that spilled out from the socket, the sudden bloom into blue air, the collective rush of hot blood, the whole disgusting spectacle spun into shape by the magical potentiality of Liquid Life.

WHAT WAS LIQUID LIFE?

Liquid Life was the marrow of salvation, the sticky heart in the swell of apocalypse. Liquid Life made every colour into One and slickened the seas like a lover. Liquid Life was the opposite of purity but the cause of all unity, because it was what happened when dead matter togethered itself at last. All the Liquid Life on Earth ran away at the Great Collapse, and now it was simply a spectre, a heavenly mighthavebeen.

AS THE OLD FOLK TUNE GOES,

Liquid Life, she stole my wife, she took her clean away
Pumped her full
Of Animal
And now she's soft as clay!

THE FIRST DOCTOR SPINS THE GLOBE WITH ONE FINGER AND SAYS,

A cloud is gathering.
I don't understand, says the second doctor. What does it want?
It thinks that the relics are Billionheir spawn, says the first doctor quietly. It thinks that if they are opened up, Liquid Life will spill out.
That's absurd.
The commonweb has never been rational.
What do they expect us to do?
Give them over. Offer them up.

The second doctor leans over and stills the spinning globe. Well, he says. Should we?

TRANSCRIPT: MEETING BETWEEN <PATIENT: ELAINE> AND <PATIENT: MAE>, ARIZONA, 18/07/3578

Elaine?

...

They wanted me to meet you.

Please talk to me, Elaine.

Please?

...

Look, you have to talk to me. We're strangers together here. Lost time-travellers.

Time-travellers.

You know what I mean.

...

I know who you are. They told me.

I know. I'm sorry.

...

Elaine, I know this is going to sound… but… well, I'm worried that we might be in danger.

...

Elaine—

What sort of danger.

Well, I've been talking to some of the clinicians at it seems that there has been a—well, not a miscommunication, but—I mean, it's quite understandable really, we must seem so strange to them, and their grasp of—well, I suppose they'd call it ancient history, if you can believe it— isn't exactly… it seems that we've been incorporated into some kind of *mythology*.

What do you mean.

They think that we were experiments performed by a sort of—sect. A sect that instigated a planetary catastrophe and then jetted off into space to start a new civilisation.

Did that happen?

Who knows? I mean, it could be pure conjecture—storytelling—but if it were true—imagine! Humans all over the galaxy! It's—

Apocalyptic.

We've been away for a long time, Elaine. There have been quite a few apocalypses since we left.

…

So what do they want to do to us?

Well, we're extremely safe in here; the clinicians have assured me that—

What do they want?

They think our bodies might harbour some sort of energy

source, none of it's particularly—

So what do they—

Well, what they want to do is to—

What?

Sacrifice us, I suppose. In some way or another.

…

Okay.

What?

Okay. That's okay.

What do you—

It's okay.

…

Look, Elaine, I don't mean to, you know, but—when you were frozen, was it all—were you—did it just feel like a very deep sleep? Mine did. Everything was pure and quiet for years and years and years. But you—

I had bad dreams. This is a bad dream.

…

…

Robert would have—

Please don't talk about him.

Elaine—

Please.

He loved you.

He left me.

He thought you were dead.
He knew it was temporary.
He couldn't have known for sure.
He knew.
…
He knew.

THE SECOND BALLAD OF ELAINE

Elaine we've a favour to ask you,
A wager to gauge from afar,
For your heartstrings are bitumen-heavy
And the lines of your palms sealed with tar.

Allow us to make the ache softer,
Allow us to make you complete,
Living forever's so easy,
But to shift and to drift is so sweet.

There's nobody here you'll be near to.
There's no-one with whom you'll be heard.
Your lover's all covered in Time now,
O, Elaine, won't you give us the word?
The light is all listless and bloodshot
And I'm animal-tired and so close

Dissolve it and hold it pieces
And give me what I want the most
O, dissolve me and hold me in pieces
And let me escape from my ghost. ◆

THE MOON WAS HALF AN APPLE

Anna Roberts

The moon was half an apple to her,
And when the clouds came, eaten.
She, a trickled-down light-stained
Fruit fly.

The sun was sycophantic and lemon-tinged father,
Crawling a pre-drawn ellipsis to the dark.
She, a sea-deep un-cored
Frog-spawned idea.

Easy does it:
Reaching to touch the sun and the moon
Leaves your underbelly exposed. ◆

PUPPET (SUSPENSION), AUDREY LEE ▸

BIOGRAPHIES
Contributors

Zehra A. reads History at Oxford. She spends her time doing anything but her degree.

Tilly Alexander is an MSt student reading English (1830-1914) at Lady Margaret Hall, Oxford. Her favourite poets include Emily Dickinson, Alice Oswald, and Ilya Kaminsky.

Solal Bauer is a second-year Human, Social, and Political Sciences student at Emmanuel College, Cambridge. His interests include late-20th-century American literature, brunch with the girls, and Kate Bush's red dress.

Charlotte Bird is a second-year Architecture student at Gonville & Caius College, Cambridge. Blurring the boundary between land and sea, her work focuses on revitalising British coastal towns, creating spaces of culture and contemplation.

Pol Bradford-Corris is a second-year History of Art student at Homerton College, Cambridge. They are interested in disrupting and layering multiple visual planes, as well as the fragmentation and reconstitution of memory.

Daniya Baiguzhayeva is a second-year English student at Emmanuel College, Cambridge. Her interviews have been featured in *Red Queen Literary Magazine* and *The Adroit Journal*, her writing in *Literary Review* and *Menacing Hedge*, among others.

Lily Bayntun-Coward is a third-year Classics student at St John's College, Cambridge. Her interests include her golden retriever, Mulberry, the colour pink and discovering much more modern Greek poetry than usual.

James Dobbyn is a second-year MSt Creative Writing student at St Anne's College, Oxford and works as a researcher for a London-based TV production company. He is writing an epic sci-fi poem inspired by Blake's prophetic books.

Oluwasemilore Delano is a third-year Architecture student at King's College, Cambridge. Her work is tethered to a daily dwelling of space, a composition of mundane moments which elaborate on the complexity of the diasporic contemporary existence. It is a subjective experience making a statement about a multifarious reality. It is nothing new or exciting, instead it is the recurring 'everyday' practises.

Kathryn Ellis is a Master's student in Cambridge. Interests include Modernist women, bodies and prose styles in nineteenth-century writing, tending houseplants and trying to avoid autofiction.

Emily is a second-year English student at Girton College, Cambridge. She is manifesting.

Cecily Fasham is a second-year English student at Gonville & Caius College, Cambridge. Against her better instincts, she writes poetry, and is interested in translation, reading-experience, and the forgotten history of women's sonnets.

Isabella Fox is a first-year English student at Murray Edwards College, Cambridge. She enjoys cold sunny days, white hydrangeas and choral singing.

Katharina Friege is a DPhil History student at St Hugh's College, Oxford. She works on notions of identity and belonging.

Groz is a first-year Modern and Medieval Languages student at Trinity Hall, Cambridge. Her praxis is mainly concerned with exploring subject self-fashioning under the scrutiny of the camera gaze—the ritual theatrics and showmanship that someone participates in front of the lens.

E. L. Hallesy is a second-year DPhil in French at New College, Oxford. She was runner-up in the 2019 Jon Stallworthy Prize for Poetry. Her interests include

Modernist representations of sound in literature and hot springs.

Olivia Healey is a third-year Zoology student at Corpus Christi college. Her interests include fantasy novels, the inner workings of birds and dying her hair ridiculous colours.

Maria Kaminska is a first-year Theology student at Christ's College, Cambridge. She is interested in modern myths and the question of inexpressibility in the literary texts. In her photography she tries to put into practice Cartier-Bresson's rule of decisive moment.

Yul HR Kang, MD, PhD, is a tenant and an international migrant in Cambridge, where he studies neuroscience as a postdoc in the Computational and Biological Learning Lab and serves as a Junior Research Fellow at Wolfson College. He illustrates concepts in neuroscience and related disciplines, as well as his life through multiple countries, with everyday objects in surreal arrangements.

Elle Lavoix is a short story writer, playwright and humanitarian worker currently based in Bamako, Mali. She is completing an MSt in Creative Writing at Selwyn College, Cambridge. Her work explores gender, power structures and vulnerabilities linked to the digital era.

Audrey Lee is a finalist at St Edmund Hall, Oxford, studying Fine Art at the Ruskin. She is enthusiastic about Tiktok dances, fish fingers (contrary to supposed vegetarianism), and starting sketchbooks she will never finish.

Alejandro Lemus-Gomez is a Davies-Jackson scholar reading Modern and Medieval Languages at St. John's College, Cambridge. Having been born in the United States to Cuban exiles, his interests are in the intersection of place and memory, intergenerational trauma, and hybrid identities. His academic work and poetry is forthcoming or has appeared in *The Afro-Hispanic Review, The Journal, storySouth, The Indiana Review Online,* and other journals.

Davide Massimo is a third year DPhil in Classics at Magdalen College, Oxford. Whenever he is not busy with dead languages and poets, he likes to venture into the realm of the living with a camera.

Sebastian McKimm is studying for an MPhil in Film and Screen Studies at Wolfson College, Cambridge. His interests include liminal states among linguistic spheres and discourses, the quest for the perfect risotto, and the art of sudden digressions.

Eli Nelson is a first-year English literature student at

Churchill College, Cambridge. Interests include God, friends, night time, ceilidh music.

Georgie Newson-Errey is a second-year English student at King's College, Cambridge. She is currently improving her juggling skills, reading a lot about witchcraft, and looking back on January 2020 with a renewed sense of nostalgia.

Rebecka Nordenlöw is a third-year English student at Lucy Cavendish College, Cambridge. Her influences include early twentieth-century Swedish literature and Middle English alliterative verse. She enjoys mountains, whiskey, and languages.

Paul Norris is an English finalist at Queens' College, Cambridge. He is interested in how poetry coexists with everyday activities and beliefs, and is currently thinking (like most people at the moment) about domestic space.

Ben Aroya Philipps is a second-year English student at Queens' College, Cambridge. He enjoys cooking and reading about food, and anything by Elizabeth Bishop.

Sona Popat is a second-year Biological Natural Sciences student at Downing College, Cambridge. She can usually be found writing about the parallels between art and science, talking about bees, and using far too many exclamation marks.

Maiss Razem is a second-year PhD Architecture student at Churchill College, Cambridge interested in designing sustainable buildings and exploring connections between humans and nature through art and photography.

Hannah Rice is a second-year English student at Lucy Cavendish College, Cambridge. Hannah is interested in how time and memory can be represented in writing.

Anna Roberts is a first-year English student at Somerville College, Oxford. Her poetry explores the surreal and the natural, mapping the strangeness of human thought onto the strangeness of the outside world.

Marnie Shutter is a second-year English student at Trinity College, Oxford. 'Willow Mellow-Wellow Wonder' was based upon the mind and antics of a rather mischievous friend, and Marnie enjoys seeking artistic puckishness, particularly within the literary works of Fernando Pessoa, Frank O'Hara, Patti Smith and August Kleinzahler.

David Swarbrick is a fourth-year Engineer at Churchill College, Cambridge. When he's not building robots or playing lacrosse, you can find him DJing, cycling, or sailing.

Imani Thompson is a first-year English student at Lucy Cavendish, Cambridge. Her interests include the politics of privilege, our relationship with nature, and daydreaming.

Kate Towsey is a third-year art historian at Trinity Hall, Cambridge. Her interests include the construction of identity through social media and by other digital means.

Pedro Valério Vieira is an Architecture and Urban Design graduate at Hughes Hall, Cambridge. Pedro's work has long followed his travels and his photographs explore how people interact with the different spaces and environments in which they find themselves.

Ben Webb is a second-year ASNC student at Peterhouse, Cambridge, where he co-edits the college's literary magazine, *The Dodo*. His interests include religion and myth, translation, and the perception of time.

Joe Wills is a second-year English student at Emmanuel College, Cambridge. He likes taking photos of people with connections to the uncommon spaces they inhabit.

Isaac Zamet is a third-year English student at Magdalene College, Cambridge. He's interested in temperature. ◆

COLLEGE SPONSORS

All Souls College, Oxford
Clare Hall, Cambridge
Exeter College, Oxford
Girton College, Cambridge
Gonville & Caius College, Cambridge
Homerton College, Cambridge
Jesus College, Cambridge
Jesus College, Oxford
Lucy Cavendish College, Cambridge
Magdalene College, Cambridge
New College, Oxford
Pembroke College, Cambridge
Peterhouse, Cambridge
Queens' College, Cambridge
The Queen's College, Oxford
Robinson College, Cambridge
St John's College, Oxford
Trinity College, Cambridge
Trinity Hall, Cambridge